"I had the privilege to get to know and love Lauren Chandler at the height of the season when God was wringing worship from her heart. I saw her cling to Him for dear life and resolve to trust Him amid terrifying circumstances. I also saw the very worship she describes in these pages surface in exquisite beauty. I am deeply grateful God put her pen to the page to share with us what He's shown her and taught her in Psalm 107. Lauren has encountered the steadfast love of God vividly and powerfully. Within these pages, we are invited to do the same. Lauren's tremendous gifting is obvious from first to last. She devours the Scriptures and makes us hungry for them, too. This is a gorgeous book. For all our sakes, I hope and trust it won't be her last."

—Beth Moore

"The steadfast love of God is a powerful balm for our souls, whether in the mundane details of daily life or in the deepest valleys through which we may be required to walk. I've watched as Lauren Chandler has clung to His faithfulness, goodness, and love in the midst of desperate places and have witnessed the sweet fruit as she has tethered her heart to the truth about His character and ways. Regardless of where you may find yourself in this season, *Steadfast Love* will be a means of sweet encouragement and grace."

—Nancy Leigh DeMoss

STEADFAST *Love*

STEADFAST

Love

PUBLISHING GROUP

NASHVILLE, TENNESSEE

Published by B&H Publishing Group
Nashville, Tennessee

Dewey Decimal Classification: 248.843
Subject Heading: CHRISTIAN LIFE \ WOMEN \ LOVE

1 2 3 4 5 6 7 8 • 20 19 18 17 16

Dedication

Acknowledgments

To my God, the Lord, who has shown me steadfast love. You are good and do good. You are worth writing about. May I never cease declaring your praise. May You ever keep me according to Your faithfulness displayed perfectly through Christ—His life, His death, and His power over it. Your grace is sufficient.

To Matt, my best friend, my favorite person, my beloved. I am glad the Lord thought it good for me to grow up with you and, if He's willing, grow old with you. I am a blessed woman. Many of the words on these pages are owed to you. I've not only sat under your faithful teaching for almost two decades, I've seen up close how much you love Him and His word with your life—the day in, day out, no-clean-white-T-shirts-in-the-drawers-but-still-seeking-to-serve-me love. You make me love Him more.

To my children, Audrey, Reid, and Norah. Thank you for your patience with this Jesus-needing Momma. Each of you are a delight to my heart, and I marvel at God's goodness in en-trusting you to me. I love you and really, really like you.

To Momma and Daddy, you were the first to believe I could actually do something like this. Who knew that little poem could turn into a book! Thank you for loving me well—pointing me to the Lover of my soul from the very beginning. I am blessed to be your daughter.

To Jennie Allen, this book may not have been written if it weren't for a lunch at La Madeleine with a woman I barely knew but am so glad to call friend now. Thank you for being boldly in love with Jesus. It's contagious.

To Ann Voskamp, thank you for your beautiful words and more beautiful soul. Your pen gives life and hope because you write from the overflow of grace and gratitude.

To Jonathan, Lisa, Grace, Pam, Rachel, Michael, and Maury, thank you for letting me write about you. Your lives have indelibly marked mine.

To Sarah, Carri, Natalie, Barkley, Kristyn, Faith, Amy, Tara-Leigh, Candice, and Courtney thank you for praying faithfully for this project and enduring the same prayer request for months on end!

To Jen Wilkin, Kelly Minter, John Piper, Tim Keller, and the team that authored the ESV Study Bible notes, thank you for faithfully mining the Scriptures for great treasure. I am among the many who have benefited from your labor—the fruit of which, I hope, is evidenced in these pages.

To Jennifer Lyell, Jana Spooner, and the team at LifeWay, thank you for your patience and encouragement, for enduring e-mails and texts, and for responding graciously!

To Doug Stanley, for lending your gifts to make this a reality. Thank you.

To Celebrate Recovery, for helping me see the chains.

Contents

Foreword

When you first meet Lauren Chandler, you wouldn't think she's a woman who's rode out a tsunami.

I met Lauren in an island of stillness up in the hill country of Texas.

We sat out in the quiet of slanting sun. Lauren spoke with this steadying calm, like the clearing surface of reflective water.

Cancer had slammed her Richter scale one unsuspecting morning, a tumor quaking her husband's brain and their whole world.

She glanced down at the cup of coffee in her hands, "No one gives you any warning what day a wave's going to slam into your whole world and everything you know is going to take a complete 180."

She looked up.

And she handed me a number right there: 107.

When everything takes a 180—take the 107. Lauren turned to Psalm 107, like a woman who'd ridden out storms was turning this key.

When I first heard Howard Ulrich talk about riding the largest tsunami of modern times, he had a coffee in his hands too. Howard had got up that morning with absolutely no warning that a monster wave, taller than the Empire State Building, would literally slam into him and his boy.

He and his eight-year-old son "Sonny" had anchored on the south side of Lituya Bay in a place called—-"Anchorage Cove."

"Some went down to the sea in ships,
doing business on the great waters . . ." (Ps. 107:23)

Howard had said: "All was smooth. It was a quiet and peaceful anchorage." There can be unwavering peace today when an uncertain tomorrow is trusted to an unchanging God.

With no notice, Howard's boat, Howard's boy, the bay, the circling mountains, the earth shook with one violent 7.8 earthquake—and forty million cubic yards of rock, ice, and coarse soil weighing ninety million tons, slammed into the drowsy bay. Fifty miles to the north, people stopped dead in their tracks, the explosion thrumming inner ear drums.

Howard stood dazed on the deck of his boat: "Out of the corner of my eye, there was an explosion of water sending up a splash seventeen hundred feet high—-and then the wave started coming."

"For he commanded and raised the stormy wind,
which lifted up the waves of the sea." (Ps. 107:25)

When God raises the winds and lifts the waves—you can always trust His hand to lift you higher—further up into Himself.

"It was a wall of water, straight up and down, about two hundred feet tall, and it was black—totally black from the soil and trees." You could see the shadows of the terror of it flash across Howard's memories. "That whole wave was traveling about seventy miles per hour—but it was strangely silent."

I've known that before—the strange silence of the encroaching crisis. I've known that too: The silence of God you hear in the midst of storms—can be the deep intimacy of God falling all around you, an intimacy that is beyond words—that will carry you through and *beyond* this storm.

"It was snapping these spruce trees along the side of the bay." Howard had shifted his coffee mug, pointed to the treed shore rising up from the bay. "They were big spruce trees, probably four hundred years old, and it was hitting them so hard, it was cutting them off at the stump."

Lauren had said that her husband had just buckled and collapsed that morning, that cancerous tumor sending out seizure shockwave after wave.

"I was looking at death—that was exactly my first thought. I didn't think we had a chance—" Howard's voice cracked. "There was no way my boat was going to make it over that wave."

Howard, eying the all-consuming wall of towering black water bearing down, threw his son a life preserver, and said, "Son—start praying."

In every storm—Your Father gives you a life preserver—and it is always His Son.

In the face of every rising wave overwhelming you—it's always turning to God's face that overwhelms you with a rising grace.

In every great crisis—let it bring out the greatness of Christ in you. *Real prayer always has eyes on* **Christ***, not the* **crisis***.*

"Then they cried to the Lord in their trouble . . ." (Ps. 107:28)

Lauren's Psalm 107, this powerfully relevant Psalm that she remarkably unfolds in these luminous, steadying pages—it speaks of four different kinds of people crying out, it speaks of all of us right there throughout Psalm 107:

• Home-seekers: *"Some wandered and were homeless."* Who isn't seeking a Home in a thousand lost and weary ways?

- Hero-seekers: *"Some sat in darkness and the deepest gloom, prisoners suffering in iron chains . . ."* Who isn't seeking a Hero to rescue from a dark suffering and save and literally set us free?
- Healer-seeker: *"Some became fools through their rebellious ways and suffered affliction because of their iniquities."* Who isn't seeking a Healer for hidden wounds?
- Hand-seeker: *"Others went out on the sea in ships . . . their courage melted away . . ."* Who isn't seeking a Hand to hold on to in the midst of the pounding waves and the ravenous storm and the frothing, drowning sea?

And it's Psalm 107's Home-seekers and Hero-seekers and Healer-seekers and Hand-Seekers—who find everything they seek in Him—Jesus—because Jesus is everything. Every single one, in spite of different stories and different storms, all simply cried: *"Then they cried to the Lord in their trouble."* The way the children of God get the unwavering, steadfast love they need in their life—is to cry out for it. Never be afraid of crying—tears deliver a singular kind of deliverance. Those who genuinely cry out—*genuinely feel His steadfast love come in.*

Because the only condition for the steadfast love of God—is that you realize can't meet any of the conditions. "All you need is need" (Tim Keller)—all you need is to cry out. *"Then they cried to the Lord . . ."*

And it happens, just like Lauren puts it memorably like this: "Sometimes He wrings the worship from our hearts." *Child—start praying.* Feel the preserving encircling of Christ around you and start praying and praising and thanking and worshipping. Stand in the rising, twisting storm—and let Him gently wring an unforgettable worship from our hearts.

Howard had showed us with the twisting of his hands, how it happened right in the face of the looming wave: "I had forty fathoms of anchor chain, and it started running out—running off the boat, came to the end—and just snapped it like a string."

Sometimes what we're holding on to isn't really an anchor for our soul—but an idol for our destruction. Sometimes when it feels like God's breaking our anchor—He's really breaking our idols—*what we were holding on to more than we were holding on to Him.*

Sometimes God allows all our anchors to break—*so we know the only unbreakable anchor we have is Him.*

"When the wave hit the boat, it shot us upward—skyward," Howard turned.

"It all drove me further up into God," Lauren turned. When this woman speaks, you hear Christ—she exudes the wisdom of one who has faced a family catastrophe—and never stopped considering the steadfast love of her Father.

That tsunami wave struck Howard's boat, struck the shore, that wave sweeping trees off a hillside at a incomprehensible height of more than 1,720 feet.

"The engine was wide open trying to get up that wave. And then it was on us," Howard nods toward Sonny.

"They mounted up to heaven; they went down to the depths;
their courage melted away in their evil plight . . ." (Ps. 107:26)

Overwhelming waves can carry you into the open arms and overwhelming love of God.

"It snapped the anchor, and the chain whipped around and hit the pilothouse door. It carried us a hundred feet up, but we couldn't see anything but water and trees. We swept up in the wave over land, up over the trees. We rode the wave as it swept us above the trees. It was pushing us backward, and I was sure it was going to break and swamp us. Then the wave was breaking. It was breaking around us, on either side, but not quite where the boat was . . ." Howard choked up.

When you feel like the pounding waves of everything might break you—look for how He's using everything to break the wave.

"And somehow" Howard shifted, stood up straighter, his eyes smiling a relief of thanksgiving, after riding that tsunami wave that roared higher than the Empire State building—"Somehow we got on top of it and to the other side"—

Yes, that, *that*: When you don't know how to get out the other side—keep pressing into Christ's side.

". . . and he delivered them from their distress . . .
He sent out his word and healed them,
and delivered them from their destruction.
Then they were glad that the waters were quiet,
and he brought them to their desired haven.
Let them thank the Lord for his steadfast love . . .
Whoever is wise, let him heed these things and consider
the great love of the LORD." (Ps. 107)

You can hear it in Lauren's words in these pages you're holding in your own hand, even as you hear the thunder of your own rising waves, what she knows from riding out her own tsunami: Wisdom isn't a function of considering great amounts of *knowledge*—it's the wise who continually consider the great, *steadfast love of God*.

And if the Home-seekers and the Hero-Seekers and Healer-seekers and the Hand-seekers—if we all want to know the reality of steadfast love of God—the brutality of the natural world will not convince, the mentality of the religious world can not persuade, and the immorality of the history of the world will not prove. Nature may let us feel close to God—but it's only knowing the nature of *God's Word* that let's us actually know God. It is only through the *Word of God* that humanity became consciously aware of *the steadfast love of God*.

It's only within the framework of creation, fall, and redemption—that the framework of a loving God makes any sense. And it's only the Word of God that says that the Creator of the World knows it's a fallen broken world, and He's breaking back into the world to redeem the whole world. You don't truly know the love of God unless you surrender, believe, and truly obey the Word of God.

The only way you can keep standing through the waves—is that you know His steadfast love through His Word.

> *"Let them thank the Lord for his steadfast love,*
> *for his wondrous works to the children of man!*
> *And let them offer sacrifices of thanksgiving,*
> *and tell of his deeds in songs of joy!" (Ps. 107)*

Lauren has lived exactly this. In the face of extreme difficulties and extreme diversity, every single one of His-seekers all receive the same extreme, steadfast love—and every single one of us are called to give the extreme sacrifice of thanksgiving. Thanksgiving isn't only a celebration when good things happen—thanksgiving is a declaration that God is good *no matter what happens.* No matter what earthquake hits, no matter what waves loom, no matter what tsunami hit on some unsuspecting day.

Since that day we met in the stillness of some Texas hill country sun—I've been anxiously and prayerfully waiting for these rare and holy words from Lauren Chandler. Waiting to hear how Psalm 107 anchored her in an uncommon wisdom through a life tsunami—because one day we're all guaranteed to wake up and it will feel like all our anchors of this world have broke.

And every line of this courageous and soulful book is like a lifeline thrown, like an unbreakable anchor for your storm, like a song to sing with a sure and brave steadiness while riding the heights the quaking storm: *Let them thank the Lord for His steadfast love.*

You feel that when you sit with Lauren Chandler, when you turn her pages of oceanic love all reflecting Christ—that, like Christ's most troubled outward life, you can feel beaten and battered by the crashing waves breaking over you—but there's an interior life that can be a sea of glass—so Christ alone is seen.

There this great calm of His steadfast love that can always be washing over a willing and surrendered soul.

—Ann Voskamp, October, 2015, the farm, Canada
author of the *New York Times* best sellers, *One Thousand Gifts: A Dare to Live Fully* and *The Greatest Gift: Unwrapping the Full Love Story of Christmas*

Introduction

I was twenty-seven years old when a friend texted me: "Read Psalm 107." She felt strongly that there was something to this passage of Scripture—that its words would weave a song in our hearts or another type of offering to encourage others. A song never came of it, but I wrote this on my little blog on the World Wide Web:

"Sometimes He wrings the worship from our hearts."

If you get the chance, read Psalm 107.

There are times when worship overflows easily and effortlessly from a heart full of gratitude and praise. Yet, there are other times when we feel we have nothing left to offer up. We are tired, or thirsty, or imprisoned in our own chains through our own devices, or caught in the waves of a tumultuous sea. This is when God wraps His eternally powerful, ultimately creative, nail-scarred hands around our hearts and squeezes with appropriate might. Our hearts painfully twist and change shape as He wrings the worship out of it. It is a deep worship. It is an honest worship. It is the worship we sometimes forget. The humble worship of crying out to God in the midst of our pain. No flowery words. No shiny faces. Not in that moment. That will come later. But for now, this is the worship He seeks—an honest plea for Him to save us.

"Then they cried to the LORD in their trouble, and he delivered them from their distress" (Ps. 107:6, 13, 19, 28).

I scrawled a picture of a heart twisting like a damp rag dripping with whimsical curls and droplets. The image has ever since burned in my mind. As I typed out the words for the book you're holding in your hands, the Lord gave me another picture: an anchor, worn but strong.

Eight years span the gap between the twisting heart and the well-worn anchor. I have known many a desert, prison, folly, and storm, and the gut-level worship they wrung from my heart. To my surprise, I found many places in Scripture where people just like me struggled through their own seasons of distress. Each were loved by God in the midst of it and delivered from it.

Psalm 107 is the first psalm of the fifth book of the Psalms. It was written about actual events. People were physically in the desert, in chains, in folly, and in the storms, and God rescued them. Troubles and rescue continue still, perhaps not in the same form but in the same spirit. Many of us have had our seasons in the desert. We've felt alone, dry, and dissatisfied. Many have felt the heavy chains of bondage, shackles that we futilely struggle against to no avail. Folly has led us to places we never thought we were capable of going. We have been shocked by our own vices. The storms come for all of us. No one escapes loss this side of heaven.

The beauty of this psalm is that there is not one season in which we have not found ourselves. It is an invitation to self-examination balanced by God-exaltation. We see ourselves with the psalmist's eyes, we recognize the ache, the sting, the heaviness; and, we identify with their cry for help. The picture of God's deliverance in each scenario encourages us to trust that He is willing and able—that there is a God who cares, who is not far off, who concerns Himself with our concerns, and who is the only One capable of rescuing us.

I invite you to scoot up a chair and lean in to hear the good news that no matter the season, no matter if we're hungry and thirsty, heavy-hearted, entangled in sin, or weathering a storm, God is the Lord of steadfast love, the anchor of our souls.

PART ONE

A Call to Worship

(PSALM 107:1–3)

Oh give thanks to the Lord, for he is good,
for his steadfast love endures forever!
Let the redeemed of the Lord say so,
whom he has redeemed from trouble
and gathered in from the lands,
from the east and from the west,
from the north and from the south.

CHAPTER ONE

The LORD of Steadfast Love

Oh give thanks to the LORD, for he is good,
for his steadfast love endures forever!

Our friend Michael Bleecker is the worship pastor at The Village Church's Flower Mound campus. We give him the hardest time about a habit of his. Thank goodness he is one of the most gracious individuals I know. This habit is why I think he's such a gifted worship leader.

Michael and his wife, Faith, are foodies. Rarely do Matt (my husband) and I find a hip new dive that they haven't already patronized, documented with photos and a detailed description, and recommended to anyone in earshot. We, however, find what we like and stick to it. Most of it is my fault. There is a Tex-Mex restaurant roughly two miles from our house that has become a new favorite. Recently, I walked in for the fourth time in two weeks and one of the waitresses greeted me with, "You sure like this place, don't you?" Adventurous in fare, we are not. Michael and Faith? The Lewis and Clark of dining-out. So when it comes to a special night out for Matt and me, one for which we prepare weeks in advance in case we get lost in the wilderness of downtown or uptown or inside-out-town Dallas, we call the Bleeckers. Never have we been disappointed. The only thing is, when Michael suggests a certain establishment, he always insists they have "the best (fill in the blank)." Every single time. It happens so much that we've started questioning him.

"But, we thought Rise had the best soufflé."

"Oh yeah, they do but this truly is the best."

Our heads turn sideways in skepticism. The problem with it all being the best is that it is semantically unfaithful. Everything can't be the best. It's not the best if it is.

Our ribbing doesn't enlighten him to that reality, he already knows it. Words just fail him. The depth of delight he has in whatever morsel he's savoring is too much for words, but he's compelled to share it with you (that is, how good it is, not the dish itself; don't get greedy).

Psalm 107 is fashioned more like a modern worship song than most of the other psalms in the book. It has a cadence, a rhythm. There's a clear refrain and the verses are easily identified. As a worship leader and songwriter, I was immediately drawn to it.

I could imagine the song leader beckoning the people to join him. His eyes are eager. He looks from face to face pleading with each lyric. He has tasted the goodness of the Lord. He has known the steadfast love of the Lord. He has traced it with his own heart in the stories passed from ancestor to ancestor and what he has discovered personally.

It's not enough for him to sing it alone. The people. They needed to know it for themselves. They needed to recite the truth. Their souls (and his) would not be satisfied until they did. This is the mark of a worship leader. This is a call to worship.

WHAT'S IN A NAME?

Names are a big deal. As soon as a pregnant friend finds out the gender of her baby, my first question is, "Do you have a name yet?" There are those who choose to wait to announce the name for understandable reasons. They want to leave room for a last-minute change. Or maybe they secretly hate monogrammed baby gifts and this gives them a good excuse. Either way, I can put myself in their shoes. The shoes I struggle to put on that other people wear comfortably are the ones who don't find out what they're having. The moment it's possible to discern the tiny parts that identify them as male or female, I'm lying on my back ready to know. I once thought it was because I'm controlling, or the nesting instinct was so strong I couldn't wait to start appointing the nursery accordingly; but now I think it goes deeper.

When I can start calling the bundle of joy stirring inside me, molding my belly into odd shapes, by name, a connection is made that I lacked before. Their names distinguish them. Instead of, "Hey, you," it's, "Well hello, Audrey (or Reid or Norah)." And in naming our children, we took care to select names that meant something desirable, not that just sounded lovely, in case they lived up to their names:

Noble strength.

Red, the color of redemption.

Torch, to light up the dark.

Names help define.

"THE LORD"

There are different names for God that He revealed to His people to distinguish and define Himself from among other gods. "The LORD" in Hebrew is *Yahweh*, the secret name for God. A name so holy and sacred the Israelites would not utter it. The psalmist in our text purposefully chooses this name to address God.

Before we dive into the meaning of Yahweh, I want to introduce you to someone and give you a warning. This person's story and the story of his people will give context to "the LORD," but it may come across as a short biblical history lesson. Don't give up. If you're new to all of this, you can find the original account in Genesis 12—50. If you know his story like the back of a felt-board character's hand, I encourage you to stay with me and ask the Lord to show you something new. Foundations are paramount to the condition of the structure, so it's important for me to lay this well for the sake of the rest of the book.

Abraham was a man called by God to leave his family, his people, and his country to go to a land the Lord promised to give him. God also told him, "I will make of you a great nation, and I will bless you and make your name great, so that you will be a blessing" (Gen. 12:2). This implied that he would have an heir, a son who would produce sons and grandsons and great-grandsons, filling the earth with God's chosen people and becoming a blessing to the whole world. Through false starts and faith-testing delays, God fulfilled His promise of a son to Abraham. His wife, Sarah, gave birth in her old age to Isaac who eventually became the father of Jacob, also known as Israel, from which we get the term "Israelites."

One of Jacob's sons, Joseph, was sold by his brothers into slavery in Egypt. Although it seemed a bleak prospect, God used the betrayal of Joseph's brothers to bring about salvation for their family. By God's favor and grace, Joseph rose from slave to overseer of Pharaoh's house. Pharaoh was only greater than Joseph in regards to the throne. When the land in which Jacob and his sons lived was depleted by famine, they were able to seek refuge in Egypt because of Joseph's gracious forgiveness and covering. All the sons of Jacob and their families "were fruitful and increased greatly; they multiplied and grew exceedingly strong, so that the land was filled with them" (Exod. 1:7).

The favor they found in Egypt did not last forever. A new king rose to power in Egypt who did not know Joseph. He looked at the Israelites not as a blessing but as a threat. So he oppressed them. They became slaves. Along with their chains, a great darkness laid on God's people. No light at the end of the tunnel, only an endlessly black corridor.

But God remembered His promise to them. He heard their cries and lit up the interminable night with a burning bush. In Exodus 3:14–15, God finally introduces Himself to Moses as "The LORD":

God said to Moses, "I AM WHO I AM." And he said, "Say this to the people of Israel, 'I AM has sent me to you.'" God also said to Moses, "Say this to the people of Israel, 'The LORD, the God of your fathers, the God of Abraham, the God of Isaac, and the God of Jacob, has sent me to you.' This is my name forever, and thus I am to be remembered throughout all generations.'"

Yahweh, I AM WHO I AM. He has no beginning and no end. He has always been and will always be. Nothing and no one made

Him. He just is. And what He is He will always be. His character is absolutely unchanging.

My children, Noble Strength (Audrey), Redemptive Red (Reid), and Torch (Norah), are a lot like me. We like to use two words that are rarely true about a person or a circumstance: "always" and "never." As you read the statements below, make sure to draw the word in italics out three times as long as the others in the sentence, almost like you're singing it.

"But you *never* let me . . ."

"But she *always* gets to . . ."

"He *never* has to . . ."

"She *always* does that . . ."

The only truth to the "always and never" statements is that we, as humans, always and never "always and never." We are never that consistent. We will always be inconsistent. God, on the other hand, can truly say He "always" and He "nevers." He is always consistent. He is never inconsistent.

In His immutability and eternal existence, He has never needed anything or anyone. He did not create humans because He was lonely. He just wanted to. He didn't call a people for Himself through Abraham, Isaac, and Jacob because He needed them to worship Him. He just decided to show His unchanging nature to and through them. And against all appearances, despite the dark and the chains, He didn't change His mind toward His people, nor did He renege on His promise to them. He showed up burning brightly in the wilderness to fulfill it.

God spoke to Moses and said to him, "I am the LORD. I appeared to Abraham, to Isaac and to Jacob, as God Almighty, but by my name the LORD, I did not make myself known to them. I also established my covenant with them to give them the land of

*Canaan, the land in which they lived as sojourners. Moreover, I have heard the groaning of the people of Israel whom the Egyptians hold as slaves, and I have remembered my covenant. Say therefore to the people of Israel, 'I am the L*ORD*, and I will bring you out from under the burdens of the Egyptians, and I will deliver you from slavery to them, and I will redeem you with an outstretched arm and with great acts of judgment. I will take you to be my people, and I will be your God, and you shall know that I am the L*ORD *your God, who has brought you out from under the burdens of the Egyptians. I will bring you into the land that I swore to give to Abraham, to Isaac, and to Jacob. I will give it to you for a possession. I am the L*ORD*.'" (Exod. 6:2–8)*

Although it appears in this section of Scripture as if Abraham, Isaac, and Jacob (the patriarchs) never knew God referred to Himself as Yahweh, it is possible that they may have called Him that in their hearts, but they had not yet experienced Him in the fullness of the name. God introduced Himself to the patriarchs and established His covenant with them as God Almighty, El Shaddai. But it was when His beloved people were enslaved, broken down, crying in their despair, wondering if God had forgotten them, that He chose to make Himself known as Yahweh, "I AM WHO I AM."

Not only am I the covenant-making God, I am the covenant-keeping God.

I will bring you out.

I will deliver you.

I will redeem you.

I will take you to be My people.

I will be your God.

I will bring you into the land.

I will give it to you for a possession.

To call God Yahweh, the LORD, at the beginning of Psalm 107 postures the heart to perceive Him as such. This isn't just any god to whom the psalmist is crying out, this is the God who doesn't give up. This is the God who heard His people's groaning and remembered His covenant with them. He sent plagues, parted seas, and displayed His strength in redeeming His people. Nothing could stand in His way, not even the grumbling of His children.

WHAT KIND OF LOVE?

Now that we know what kind of God is being called upon in this psalm, it is good to know what motivates Him, what fuels His actions toward His people. The answer to this question is found in verse 1. Most translations of the Bible use "steadfast love" (or a variation of it) to interpret the Hebrew word *hesed*, and that's what is found here in Psalm 107.

Hesed is a term not easily encapsulated in English. Various versions of the Bible and various appearances of the word in each version translate it into "faithfulness," "goodness," "kindness," "loyalty," "mercy," and "steadfast love." The simplest definition, however, is "loyal love." It is the committed, unchanging, loving determination of the Lord who will never give up on those whom He has chosen for Himself.

The use of the word always involves two parties, "whether between family members (Gen. 20:13), a host and guest (Gen. 19:19), friends (1 Sam. 20:8, 14), or a sovereign and his subjects (2 Sam. 2:5)."[1] Among human relationships, there is a mutuality inferred, an action and a response. *Hesed* is not just emotive, it is active. It "always entails practical action on behalf of another . . ."[2] Another element of *hesed* is its enduring nature. It is a cord that runs continuously, binding two individuals or groups together.

Kindness and Redemption

The book of Ruth paints *hesed,* shown from one human to another, beautifully. At the opening of this comparatively small portion of Scripture, Naomi's once brimming cup is drained like the parched ground in her hometown. Her family is forced to move to a foreign land. But even there, the famine finds her. Not long into their sojourn, her husband dies, leaving her with two sons. They take wives from among the foreigners but lose their own lives shortly after. Naomi exchanges two sons for two daughters-in-law, Ruth and Orpah. She urges them to make new lives, to leave her in lament, throwing the ashes of her life on her head. Ruth refuses. She makes a *hesed* vow:

> *"Do not urge me to leave you or to return from following*
> *you. For where you go I will go, and where you lodge I*
> *will lodge. Your people shall be my people, and your God*
> *my God. Where you die I will die, and there will I be*
> *buried. May the* Lord *do so to me and more also if any-*
> *thing but death parts me from you."* (Ruth 1:16–17)

Committed love.

Active and enduring.

The words Ruth speaks are not in vain. She proceeds to prove them by seeking out food and favor for them both. She finds it in the fields and person of Boaz. In God's providence, it is revealed that Boaz is qualified to be Ruth's kinsman-redeemer. This means that he is a close enough relative to Naomi to fulfill two legal practices listed in the Law of Moses: property redemption and the "levirate" marriage. Property redemption entails a relative of the deceased (Ruth's husband, Mahlon) acquiring his land to keep it in the family. A "levirate" marriage is when a childless widow marries her husband's brother (in this case, a distant relative) in order to produce an heir to the deceased's property.

Although Boaz had some legal legs on which to stand in becoming kinsman-redeemer, he was not obligated to do so. There was a relative closer to Naomi, and the Law of Moses did not require both the property redemption and the marriage. Boaz was moved to show kindness, *hesed,* in redeeming both.

In the same way, Ruth was not required to show *hesed* to Naomi in staying with her, or marrying her relative in order to keep her husband's property in his name and belonging to his heir, but she did. Boaz took Ruth to be his wife and fathered a son whom they named Obed, who was the grandfather of David, in the line of Jesus Christ. In the closing scene of the book, Naomi is praising God with Obed on her lap, rocking redemption in her arms.

In telling the story of Naomi, Ruth, and Boaz, God displays the inextricable link between *hesed* and redemption. At its beginning, Naomi is stripped of everything valuable to her. She is so grieved, she demands people call her "bitter." But in the end and all along the way, steadfast love is shown and her losses are redeemed. If imperfect people like Ruth and Boaz can be so moved by *hesed* to redeem the broken and barren places, how much more will a holy God show His steadfast love by redeeming His people? Especially when it is a part of His self-description?

ABOUNDING IN STEADFAST LOVE

In Exodus 34:6–7, God used *hesed* to describe Himself. Let me set the stage first. Remember, the LORD made Himself known to His people as Yahweh, "I AM," by choosing His servant Moses to deliver them from the oppression of the Egyptians. He led them out with great signs and wonders, plagues, and the parting of the sea. He provided a pillar of cloud to lead them by day and a pillar of fire by night. When their stomachs and hearts grumbled for food, He provided heavenly bread, manna. Water flowed from a rock to quench their thirst. With only manna and quail to sustain them, they prevailed against the Amalekites by His power.

Then, the LORD called Moses up to Mount Sinai to record the Law for the sake of His people as they marched into the Promised Land. While he was gone, the people lost patience and fashioned a god that seemed good to them, a golden calf made from the plunder of Egypt. Moses descended from the top of the mountain with the stone tablets containing the Ten Commandments—the very words of God written in the very handwriting of God (Exod. 32:16). In his justified anger, Moses "threw the tablets out of his hands and broke them at the foot of the mountain" (Exod. 32:19), just as the people had broken the very first commandment, "You shall have no other gods before me." He burned the calf, crushed it into powder, scattered it on the water, and made the people drink it. Afterward, a period of confession, repentance, and cleansing commenced. Moses interceded on behalf of the people and received his request from the LORD that His presence would go with them. Moses asked Him to show him His glory, and He did so in a way that preserved Moses' life. The LORD instructed Moses to, once again, cut tablets from stone. And once again, He wrote His very words on them. Then it says in Exodus 34, starting in verse 5:

The LORD descended in the cloud and stood with him there,
and proclaimed the name of the LORD. The LORD passed before
him and proclaimed, "The LORD, the LORD, a God merciful
and gracious, slow to anger and abounding in steadfast

> love *and faithfulness, keeping* steadfast love *for thousands, forgiving iniquity and transgression and sin, but who will by no means clear the guilty, visiting the iniquity of the fathers on the children and the children's children, to the third and the fourth generation."* (Exod. 34:5–7, emphasis added)

Of all the descriptors God could have used to describe Himself (holy, just, or righteous), He chose merciful, gracious, slow to anger, faithful, and abounding in steadfast love. He gave the Law and not ten seconds after He picked up His heavenly stylus from sacred stone did the people break it. And just like their father and mother, Adam and Eve, they dealt blame to whoever fit the bill. Sin upon sin. The LORD had every right to say, "I'm done. That's it." But He didn't. Instead, He demonstrated His *hesed*—His loyal, covenant-keeping love. He invited Moses to come near and intercede on behalf of the people. He granted Moses' request to let His presence remain with them. And He started over again. New tablets. Another chance. Mercy and forgiveness on thousands.

Heavenly Hesed

This is where *hesed* between humans and *hesed* from God toward His people differs. The mutuality of *hesed* humanly speaking is not the same with God. Even though Ruth freely showed kindness to Naomi, she mutually benefited from the wisdom and encouragement Naomi had to offer. And although Boaz freely showed kindness to Ruth and Naomi, he benefited by acquiring property, producing an heir, and continuing his own bloodline. God, however, needs nothing from us (Acts 17:25). Although the LORD requires faith and obedience from His people, He knows we are but dust and prone to wander, every one of us.

So, He made a way. The Way's shadow is cast long over the account in Exodus. There was a people created in the image of God for the display of His glory. But in their impatience and brokenness, they fashioned a replacement with their own hands. The law was broken. Instead of stone tablets breaking at the foot of a mountain, a Body was broken on a cross atop a holy hill. Like Moses, the LORD interceded for the rebellious people. For "we have this as a sure and steadfast anchor of the soul, a hope that enters into the inner place behind the curtain, where Jesus has gone as a forerunner on our behalf" (Heb. 6:19–20). He gives, and becomes, another chance for us. Jesus embodies *hesed*. We know *hesed* because of Jesus.

By faith, we are invited to respond. We are beckoned to drop this anchor of *hesed* in our souls. To say, *I am guilty of trading the real God for a fake one; but You, oh God, have made a way according to Your steadfast love, Your* hesed, *through Jesus' perfect life on earth, death on the cross, and resurrection from the dead.*

DROPPING ANCHOR

What we choose to use as our anchor determines how well we will weather the seasons of life. Imagine hoisting a rope tied to a brick over the side of an ocean liner and saying, "That'll hold." Anyone in her right mind would signal the Coast Guard and be on the next boat back to shore. The brick will sink and have the appearance of stability, but the first steady current would sweep it away.

I have had my share of faux-anchors—things, people, talents, abilities, statuses, even good deeds—that felt like they would hold but without exception, each failed me. God has graciously used seasons in the desert, in chains, in folly, and in the storm to expose the weaknesses of my anchor impostors. He unties the frail rope from the measly brick and replaces it with His *hesed* chain tied to the anchor of Yahweh, the Great "I AM," the One who will never fail.

As the Lord invites you to see and know His faithfulness in showing you steadfast love, I invite you to peer into places where I have seen and known Him to be so. I must confess, it's not always pretty. There have been tears, there have been wounds, there have been downright ugly cries, but too much is at stake to not be vulnerable with you. Whether you know it or not, there is an enemy of our souls who hates steadfast anchors and loves to deceive us into trusting faux-anchors. But, he doesn't have the last say. His desire to decimate is nothing compared to the steadfast love of the Lord. As we drop the anchor, we steady ourselves for an opposing current.

CHAPTER TWO

The God Who Redeems

Let the redeemed of the LORD say so,
whom he has redeemed from trouble,
and gathered in from the lands,
from the east and from the west,
from the north and from the south.

As I type this, ISIS (the Islamic State of Iraq and Syria), a jihadist faction in Iraq, is systematically killing and driving out Christians from their homes. Men, women, and children are being beheaded and viciously murdered. The enemy of these Christians seems obvious. They're the ones with their fingers on the trigger, their eyes looking through the scope straight at them. There is, however, a more insidious enemy to these Christian men and women and even those who make up ISIS.

He showed up early in the story of the world, and early on, he showed his cards. Three chapters into the Bible, he pokes his scrawny neck through the pages of history.

Now the serpent was the most cunning of all the wild animals that the LORD God had made. He said to the woman, "Did God

> *really say, 'You can't eat from any tree in the garden'?" The*
> *woman said to the serpent, "We may eat the fruit from the trees*
> *in the garden. But about the fruit of the tree in the middle of the*
> *garden, God said, 'You must not eat it or touch it, or you will die.'"*
> *"No! You will not die," the serpent said to the woman. "In fact,*
> *God knows that when you eat it your eyes will be opened and*
> *you will be like God, knowing good and evil." Then the woman*
> *saw that the tree was good for food and delightful to look at, and*
> *that it was desirable for obtaining wisdom. So she took some*
> *of its fruit and ate it; she also gave some to her husband, who*
> *was with her, and he ate it. Then the eyes of both of them were*
> *opened, and they knew they were naked; so they sewed fig leaves*
> *together and made loincloths for themselves.* (Gen. 3:1–7 HCSB)

The spirit of the serpent is known by another name—Satan. Despite our culture's caricature, he doesn't sport a red suit with a spaded tail and pitchfork. And, he's not entirely repulsive. Even in the interaction with Eve, the serpent sidles up next to her and speaks gently. His questions aren't immediately offensive or inappropriate. He just plants a subtle seed of doubt, pats the soil firm, and finds it fertile.

Other places in Scripture describe him as disguising himself "as an angel of light" (2 Cor. 11:14). He's a fair-weather friend with kind eyes who slips you an arsenic-laced slice of apple pie. It goes down sweet but sits heavy, reaching its fingers 'round in a stranglehold.

"Did God *really* say? I'm really just asking for clarity."

And his next favorite tactic is to sensationalize what God has made clear: "You can't eat from *any* tree in the garden? Because that just sounds unreasonable."

Feeling the heat of the interrogator's lamp shining squarely on her, Eve faltered. She added to God's original and only command in the garden: "And the LORD God commanded the man, saying, 'You may surely eat of every tree of the garden, but of the tree of the knowledge of good and evil you shall not eat, for in the day that you eat of it you shall surely die'" (Gen. 2:16–17).

The command was given directly to Adam, but the Bible doesn't say whether God told Eve also or if Adam relayed the message. We're not sure if Adam botched communicating this important piece of information, or if Eve misunderstood. Whichever is true, what God truly said was twisted. That's where the enemy likes to keep us, believing God said something He really didn't say.

Once he coaxed Eve into reciting the half-truth, he came in for the kill.

"You won't surely die! How preposterous! God is just holding out on you! He's afraid that you will become like Him!"

The irony is thick. God was never afraid Adam and Eve would become like Him, He already made them to be like Him (Gen. 1:26)! They were made in His image, to bear His image, to reflect His image to the ends of the earth! The enemy delights in leading us to believe something about God that isn't true. He baits us to question His character.

What else does he have up his sleeve? He appeals to our flesh. Eve saw that the fruit on the tree looked pretty enough to eat and she just happened to be hungry. The fruit had a desirable side effect to boot: wisdom. The last thing she wanted to be was a hungry fool. To be played a fool is humiliating; the enemy preys on this fear.

THE HAND OF THE ENEMY

So what does he have in his hand?

Card one: Pretend to be a friend.

Card two: Question God's Word.

Card three: Question God's character.

Card four: Appeal to our flesh.

Card five: Death.

He is always set on death. And he will always lie to get us there. He is a thief who comes to "steal and kill and destroy" (John 10:10). He knows if we can get our mind set on what we feel like we need, what we deserve, that which is apart from God, death follows closely behind. "For to set the mind on the flesh is death" (Rom. 8:6).

The fruit from the tree of the knowledge of good and evil didn't dramatically drop from Eve's and Adam's cold, dead hands. What the serpent told them was only partly true. They didn't die immediately. The fatal bite just set into motion the process of dying. Eden never knew death until that very moment.

Death didn't come alone; he brought a friend: shame. For the first time, Adam and Eve saw that they were naked and this caused shame. They had to cover themselves. Isn't it interesting that the serpent played on Eve's fear of being shamed by being made a fool, when in reality he was setting her up for the most humiliating point of her life? He plays dirty. Always.

And with death and shame came guilt. Adam and Eve were guilty of breaking Eden's only rule. Satan did all he could to draw them to betray God, but in the end the decision was theirs. Satan can tempt but he can't make you sin. "The devil made me do it" is his lie. He has power but not that much.

The enemy has played his usual hand with me. He starts with a seemingly innocent question: "What would you do if (insert a particular fear)?" One of my greatest fears is that something would happen to Matt and I would be left a widow and our three children fatherless.

He lays down card two: "Didn't God say He wouldn't let bad things happen to His children?" The answer is no. "Didn't God say He won't give you more than you can handle?" Again, no. He said He will "provide the way of escape" from temptation, that we may be able to endure it (1 Cor. 10:13). He has said He will be with me (Matt. 28:20), He will work all things for my good (Rom. 8:28), and He has defeated the greatest danger to my soul—sin (Rom. 5:8–11). But there are days when I forget His promises. Days when I'm worn down and skittish, afraid the smallest shadow brings imminent doom and all I want is to live a pain-free life.

The enemy slithers in and edges his third card within my line of sight: "Can you really call Him good if He takes good things away from you?" The right answer? There is only One who is good (Matt. 19:17). He defines what is good. If He does take what is good away, it must be because it's not what's best for all involved. But there are days when I confuse what's good with Who is good. I will grip knuckles white on "the what" instead of clinging desperately to the Who.

"But if You're really good, God," I say, "You would let me have this. You would want this for me. Since it seems You don't, You must not love me. You must not truly be good."

Card four: "Don't you think you should draw up a 'plan B'? Just in case God doesn't come through for you?"

I've misunderstood His promises and traded who He really is for my idea of who He is. My flesh screams, "You have to fend for yourself!" The enemy stands behind me, massaging the knots in my flesh, readying me for the fight.

"That's right. He said He wouldn't let bad things happen to you. Can He really be good? Can He really be trusted? Don't be fooled again!"

Card five.

Devising "plan B" focuses all of my energy and thoughts on doing whatever it takes to live apart from God. And this alienates me from reality because life truly can't be found outside of Him. My pride says I can do this thing called life on my own. Scripture tells me that I become scattered in the thoughts of my heart (Luke 1:51). Such schism disconnects me from those around me. A type of death comes into my relationships. I can't maintain my relationships when all I'm focusing on is how I can achieve plan B. With the particular fear of losing my husband, I will find myself drawing away instead of toward him out of protection. Death.

BUT GOD

If I continued to fail to acknowledge God, if I never repented of the sin of pride, I would prove that I never really trusted Him and would be found dead in my trespasses and sins.

And you were dead in the trespasses and sins in which you once walked, following the course of this world, following the prince of the power of the air, the spirit that is now at work in the sons of disobedience—among whom we all once lived in the passions of our flesh, carrying out the desires of the body and the mind, and were by nature children of wrath, like the rest of mankind. But God, being rich in mercy, because of the great love with which he loved us, even when we were dead in our trespasses, made us alive together with Christ—by grace you have been saved—and raised us up with him and seated

> *us with him in the heavenly places in Christ Jesus, so that in*
> *the coming ages he might show the immeasurable riches of*
> *his grace in kindness toward us in Christ Jesus.* (Eph. 2:1–7)

Do you see it? All the elements are there. Death comes from following the prince of the power of the air (Satan). The way he walks and those who follow him. Disobedience. To what does he appeal? The passions of our flesh. And then two words interject. Two words that change everything.

But God.

Even in the garden, when the enemy thought he had God right where he wanted Him, when he bet everything on his seemingly indomitable hand, God pulled up a chair and laid down a royal flush. He called for Adam and Eve. He sought them out fully knowing what had transpired. He found them scrambling to cover themselves. He gave them the chance to fess up without blame-shifting. And like children caught in the act, they pointed fingers and wagged tongues, "But she . . . but he . . ."

But God.

He is a good, just, and loving God. Although it must have pained Him to dispense justice, it's what was right. He pronounced their punishment—Adam's, Eve's, and the enemy's. In the serpent's sentence He whispered hope of the coming rescue, "I will put enmity between you and the woman, and between your offspring and her offspring; he shall bruise your head, and you shall bruise his heel" (Gen. 3:15). There would be One coming whom the enemy would harm but not enough to keep Him from fatally wounding him in return.

But God.

Before Adam and Eve were driven from Eden with heads low and hearts heavy, God exhibited His *hesed*. In unmerited kindness and love, He shadowed future redemption. In desperation, to cover their guilt and shame, Adam and Eve had sewn fig leaves together. This probably looked much like the scene when my youngest dressed herself for the first time. Multiple layers of shirts worn backward, pants on the right leg but unzipped and unsnapped, shoes on the wrong feet with laces spilling over. The right idea but insufficient in so many ways. Adam and Eve knew they needed to be covered but all they could come up with just wasn't enough. God compassionately made a covering for them. In order to do so though, something had to die. There had to be a sacrifice of one life for another. An animal was killed, its blood drained, its hide flayed. Adam and Eve? Covered.

One day, on this side of Eden, Jesus would be the ultimate sacrifice, the covering for those who would be called children of God. His perfection would swallow up their imperfection, the source of their guilt and shame. For those who would trust Him, He would step in and turn over the table, ending the game with the enemy.

He has done that for me. When I think all is lost, that I've blown it again and wonder how can He put up with me, and I hear the enemy snickering in triumph, Jesus taps me on the shoulder and stands in my place. He reminds me that only He can end it. And He will, by crushing the enemy's head.

INEFFECTIVE ANCHORS, INEFFECTIVE IMAGERS

As sure as God has a plan for us, the enemy has his own. But we are not unaware of his schemes. We know the hand he will play. With each card he lays down, he draws us toward destruction. He does everything he can to convince us God's steadfast love is weak and deficient. He calls into question the integrity of the anchor of our souls.

Can it really hold?

Are you sure this is the right anchor for this vessel?

If the enemy can get us to forsake the true anchor for a substitute, he has us right where he wants us: ineffective and defeated, adrift on a tumultuous sea, thrown by every wave, aimless and in danger of breaking into pieces on the rocky shore. Why is it important to him for us to be ineffective?

If you'll remember in the account with Eve, the serpent suggested God was afraid that she and Adam would become like Him. But that was God's plan all along. He made them both in His image. To bear His attributes on earth. To be His representatives in the world.

The enemy hates God and since he knows he has no power over Him, he believes the next best move is to mar God's image in His image bearers. He decides to make ineffective imagers by baiting them with ineffective anchors.

You see, he wanted to test our faithfulness. Would we be content being like God or would we want to *be* God? Would we trust God to be our anchor or would we scoff at the very need for one? His gamble paid off. Adam and Eve took the bait. We too have taken the bait. Now all that was made to image God is broken, marred.

In the beginning, God tasked man to represent Him:

And God blessed them. And God said to them, "Be fruitful and multiply and fill the earth and subdue it and have dominion over the fish of the sea and over the birds of the heavens and over every living thing that moves on the earth." And God said, "Behold, I have given you every plant yielding seed that is on the face of all the earth, and every tree with seed in its fruit. You shall have them for food. And to every beast of the earth

*and to every bird of the heavens and to everything that creeps
on the earth, everything that has the breath of life, I have given
every green plant for food." And it was so.* (Gen. 1:28–30)

We are meant to show His attributes in how we are fruitful and multiply and how we fill and subdue the earth. He gave us the ability to reflect His creativity by the miracle of human conception and birth and by creating pieces of art or building something with our hands or constructing ideas that improve our life and others' lives.

Writing songs is one of the most exhilarating and yet agonizing processes for me. Being a firstborn artist is a cruel joke. My firstborn self critiques and overly edits what the artist in me creates. Firstborn self says, "It's not worth doing if it's not perfect." So as soon as a lyric or melody materializes, the perfectionist picks and questions, and a half-written song sits on the shelf accumulating dust, waiting for the artist to overcome. Sometimes she does, but most of the time it is an intense struggle between the two. When I can finally get them on the same page and a song emerges victoriously, I might as well be Rocky on the steps in Philadelphia, fists in the air, bouncing from one foot to the other.

Although there is much merit in my firstborn tendency to offer something polished and whole, I can easily fall into fear and pride. If the song is less than what I want, I will bemoan:

I'm not good enough.

This isn't really what I'm supposed to be doing.

What's the point, really?

I should be better than this.

And if the song is better than I could imagine, I will proudly puff larger than a marshmallow in the microwave:

Man, I'm good.

I deserve some special position or recognition.

More often than not, though, fear wins. I tend toward defeat and self-pity more than accomplishment and self-praise. It's weak pride, really. I buy into the lie that I should be more than what I am. I am convinced that the giftedness given to me by God isn't enough; it should look like hers, or his.

I anchor my soul to what I am and what I can do and am paralyzed, rendered impotent. Ineffective anchor. Image marred.

When the Spirit eventually confronts me with my pride, He gives me the chance to do it differently. I get the opportunity to confess my unbelief, to say that I questioned God's good purpose in how He made me. I admit to Him that I want to *be* Him more than I want to be *like* Him. I also get the pleasure of thanking Him for how He has made me, how He delights in my using the gifts He's given me to make much of Him. The true anchor is restored and I am freed to be effective.

I cease taking myself too seriously and lift my offering before others. They may make adjustments but my heart is steady. Their criticism serves to make the song better so that it may communicate and connect more clearly to the listener. Or, they may applaud and my heart is ready. Their praise refracts through my heart into praise of the Source. Listeners are blessed and drawn to join in the praising.

A LION ON A LEASH

There are varying degrees of the enemy's opposition. When I come against him in imaging God through songwriting, it usually costs me little. Tears may be shed. Hours wasted. Sometimes though, he is ruthless. He was ruthless with Job.

Job was an upstanding citizen. In fact, he was more. Scripture says he was "blameless and upright, one who feared God and turned away from evil" (Job 1:1). This man wasn't just a "good ol' boy"; he was a good man. He wasn't like the man who shows up to church on Easter and Christmas to get his wife off his back and to appease "the Man Upstairs." No, he worshiped God body and soul. He knew God and God knew him.

One day, God noticed Satan tagging along with the "sons of God" who were presenting themselves before the Lord. He turned Satan's attention to Job.

And the Lord *said to Satan, "Have you considered my servant*
Job, that there is none like him on the earth, a blameless and
upright man, who fears God and turns away from evil?" (Job 1:8)

At this point in the story, if I'd been Job and if I was privy to the conversation happening in the heavenlies, I would have opted out. I would have said, "Lord, thank You for the incredibly high vote of confidence, but I'm afraid You've got the wrong person."

Job wasn't aware of the interaction between God and Satan. I wonder what he would have done if he had been. Whatever he would have said or done, according to his reputation, he would have been blameless in his reaction.

Satan looked at the wealth of Job, his abundance of children, livestock, land, and possessions, and retorted, "Of course he's blameless and upright and fears You. You have given him all this stuff; You coddle him. I bet if You take away all his stuff, he'll curse You to Your face."

The Lord granted Satan the power to stretch his hand against Job, but He gave him parameters. Job's possessions, belongings, and even family were open to destruction, but Job's person and body were untouchable. If you give Satan an inch, he'll take a mile, unless you're the Lord; in that case, he'll take the full measure of whatever he's given. Satan utterly destroyed Job's estate. He killed his children, slaughtered his livestock, but left his wife alive who eventually looked on Job with contempt and bitterly advised him to "curse God and die" (Job 2:9). Insult to injury. When my husband preaches out of this section of Job, he suggests maybe Job should have traded his wife for one of the camels. It would have been a good trade!

I digress.

The point isn't the decimation but Job's dedication. The blood of his children had yet to dry before he proved Satan wrong. He tore his robe in mourning and then blessed the Lord saying, "Naked I came from my mother's womb, and naked shall I return. The LORD gave, and the LORD has taken away; blessed be the name of the LORD" (Job 1:21).

At first blush one might gasp at Job's assigning the taking to the Lord. But the very next verse says, "In all this Job did not sin or charge God with wrong" (Job 1:22). What's more astonishing is Job's trust in the Lord and intimate knowledge of His sovereignty. He didn't charge God with wrongdoing; he made clear who ultimately has the power of life and death, pain and blessing—the Lord. He trusted that God would only let something into his life for his good and God's glory. He knew this:

God sets the limits of Satan's power to cause pain. Our God is not frustrated by the power and subtlety of Satan. Satan cannot make a move without the permission of God almighty. He may be a lion. But he is a lion on a leash. And

God reins him in or gives him slack according to God's own sovereign purposes.[1]

What were God's "sovereign purposes" in letting Satan sift Job? To show His great power and worth. This may sound like a narcissistic power trip. You may be asking yourself, "Really God? You have to pick on some poor guy named Job so that You can feel power and worth? No thanks!"

It's only narcissistic if it's not true. God is most powerful and most worthy. Period. God lent Satan the power to take every faux-anchor from Job—his wealth, his family, his health, even his righteous reputation. The only thing Satan did not and could not get his grubby hands on was God's steadfast love toward Job. God loved Job enough to show him how He alone can sustain.

Even though God allowed Job to be tested, He didn't leave him in devastation. He restored the fortunes of Job, giving him twice as much as He had before. More importantly, He gave Job the chance to experience Him as the God who redeems. And this experience Job did not keep to himself. He imaged God's redemption through telling his story. He gave God glory in his suffering and his restoration. Authentic anchor, effective imager.

God is gathering a people for Himself from all over that have known Him as Job knew Him. No one is too far. No season too difficult. God can redeem anyone and anything.

Job is an example of how Satan can play his usual hand with us and lose. He can tempt us to question God's Word and His character. He can strip us of the life we know and incite us to forsake faith in God for faith in ourselves or another lesser anchor. But he is only a pawn in the hand of the Lord.

We must keep this in view as we meditate on the rest of Psalm 107. Some of what we see will shock us. We'll insist that surely there are seasons beyond redemption. My exhortation to you? Remember Job. Remember God's steadfast love to him.

PART TWO

The Desert

(PSALM 107:4–9)

Some wandered in desert wastes,
finding no way to a city to dwell in;
hungry and thirsty,
their soul fainted within them.
Then they cried to the LORD in their trouble,
and he delivered them from their distress.
He led them by a straight way
till they reached a city to dwell in.
Let them thank the LORD for his steadfast love,
for his wondrous works to the children of man!
For he satisfies the longing soul,
and the hungry soul he fills with good things.

CHAPTER THREE

Hungry and Thirsty

Some wandered in desert wastes,
finding no way to a city to dwell in;
hungry and thirsty,
their soul fainted within them.

In my mind, Africa was where the most dedicated of American Christians boldly spent their lives as missionaries. Its intimidating landscape, treacherous fauna, and exotic culture seemed in stark contrast to my little east Texas hometown. When Matt and I received an invitation to travel to South Sudan to support the work of an indigenous church, we enthusiastically accepted. I wanted to see with my own eyes what I could only imagine.

What I found in Africa far exceeded my expectations. The people were warm, generous, beautiful, and full of convicting faith. The scenery was equally inviting. One mental snapshot that has stuck with me over the years was taken not on the ground in Sudan but from the air above the Sahara.

Four hours into our eight-hour flight from Amsterdam to Entebbe, Uganda, I rested my head against the window. Immediately, I lifted my head in concern as I peered down to the surface below. Bleached waves stretched endlessly beneath me. What sort of body of water were we flying over? I had grown so accustomed to seeing the Atlantic from the previous flight that my eyes deceived me. This was no ocean; it was the desert, imposing and desolate.

I had never seen anything like it. I had always joked that the Lord sent me to the desert for college. Majestic pine trees were replaced with scrubby mesquites, gentle hills with an uninterrupted horizon (aside from a mesa to the south and the Bank of America building downtown). Abilene, Texas was an oasis compared to what I found outside the airplane window.

The older I get, the more fears I have to confront in my mind. Childlike ignorance can be blissfully peaceful. As a child I rarely watched the evening news and hardly heard horror stories involving traumatic, real-life experiences. But as an adult, I can name too many tragedies and accounts of downed airplanes. It's no surprise then that I panicked at the sight of the Sahara.

What if we crashed?

How quickly could help arrive if we survived? I can't see anything for hundreds of miles!

My overactive imagination placed me as a weary traveler swallowed by a sea of beige. No companion to be found except the ornery camel that spits at me from time to time (see what I mean?). Sad, desperate, and utterly alone.

THE MARKS OF THE DESERT

Nothing brings comfort in the desert. There's nary a shade tree. Sand settles in every crevice of your person and possessions. No civilization as far as the eye can see. Water? Even more scarce.

Two elements that characterize a spiritual desert are loneliness and longing. You can feel lonely without being alone. In fact, loneliness can be intensified when you are completely surrounded.

It would seem that feeling alone could be easily remedied by not being alone. But it's not. And it's acutely evident when you're among the people whom you love and treasure most and still you simply can't connect. An ache nags within wherever you go. All you really want is to not feel alone. You want someone to know exactly what and how you're feeling in a place so deep inside that even you can't seem to get at it; your own words fail to describe it. You seek a city, a connection, but find no way to it.

Along with a wild imagination, I have vivid and frequent dreams. Some are the result of bad pizza, others have depth and meaning. There's one recurring dream that always sends me into an anxiety attack. In the dream, I need to make an urgent call. I search desperately for my phone and fetch it from my purse. As I attempt to make the call, it becomes evident something is wrong. The apps on my iPhone move and I can't find the green square with the receiver icon. I blame my five-year-old. *Surely she somehow deleted it!* No problem, there must be a way around it. I can instruct Siri to make the call for me. I hold down the home button. No Siri. Nothing. Nada.

Now, this dream has evolved. As a kid, before cell phones were fancied to be less than the size of a piece of luggage, I was making calls from a cutting-edge cordless phone. The keys were all in the right place, but I kept hitting the wrong numbers. I'd have to hit the button to hang up and try over and over (and over) again.

The apprehension that I feel in that dream is much like the desperation I experience when I'm alone in the desert. I want to make a connection. I want to find a city, somewhere safe and populated. But no matter how much I try, I just can't.

Although human contact seems unattainable, I conclude at least God's ear must be available. But my prayers rise from my helpless heart and knock against the brass heavens. I know He's there but at a distance. The Scriptures, once a source of unending encouragement, stare straight back at me with little comfort. Old standby texts fall flat. The Word—"living and active, sharper than any two-edged sword"—feels about as serrated as a butter knife (Heb. 4:12).

The loneliness is compounded by hunger and thirst, a longing without the hope of fulfillment. My mind's eye pictures a scene from an '80s film, *The Three Amigos*. The camera hones in on the blazing sun and then cuts to Lucky Day (Steve Martin), Dusty Bottoms (Chevy Chase), and Ned Nederlander (Martin Short), wilting on horseback beneath its oppressive heat. Their exhaustion and perilous nearness to heat stroke is compounded by their flamboyant garb: wool jackets and trousers emblazoned with sequins. They're more suited for a Hollywood back lot than a Mexican wasteland. The trio stops to achieve some sort of relief by way of canteen.

Lucky comes into view first. He lifts the canteen to his lips and a few drops of water fall on his burning tongue. Hardly enough to drown a mosquito. Lucky sighs in disappointment.

The camera pans to Ned. He twists off the top to the canteen, with the same hopeful longing as Lucky, but is even more dismayed by what he finds. With the bottle hoisted above, he opens his mouth in anticipation, but all he comes up with is a swallow full of sand. He hangs his head in utter dejection.

Finally, it's Dusty's turn. Just like Lucky and Ned, he hastily draws his canteen from the saddlebag. Unlike his amigos, his canteen is an unending spring. He can barely keep up with the gushing stream. He gulps until satisfied, letting water run down the sides of his mouth, gurgling and swishing the excess. Eventually his thirst becomes so quenched that he tosses the remnant to the ground, water seeping into the cracked earth. He's not done though. The water did nothing for his dehydrated lips, so he uses his pinky to carefully dab balm all over them, smacking and simultaneously, yet inadvertently, mocking his partners' thirst.

Dusty feels the other two looking on incredulously, so he comes to his senses and offers, "Lip balm?"

The desert's like that. Everything inside you longs for comfort and relief but all you seem to come up with is a few drops of water at best or a mouth full of sand at worst. Meanwhile, it appears everyone else is enjoying every longing fulfilled. You look to your right, fulfillment. To your left, satisfaction. In the space you occupy? Lack.

Lament

Few things sap my sanity more than the incessant complaining of my children. Dear Lord, thank You that You are so much more gracious to me in my complaining than I am in my children's! Seldom is it about something they actually need. Mostly there's some want that they've confused with a need.

Mom, I neeeed this Lego set! (Like an octopus needs another tentacle.)

I have to have this saddle pad. (Never mind the one we bought two months ago.)

But my dollhouse needs more dolls to live in it! They put it on the market and a new family is moving in! (She didn't really say that but can't you just imagine it?)

I'll admit, I'm not as stalwart as Matt. I cave way too often and I kick myself every time. They wear me down, people! Steadfast in their petitions, yes, they are.

Complaining is not the same thing as lamenting. To complain is to express dissatisfaction with something you feel that you deserve but don't necessarily need. To lament is to mourn the loss of something real, something you once had but enjoy no longer. You acknowledge the loss without demanding it back. You humbly desire its return while knowing there's no merit in you alone having it.

Scripture is full of laments. A whole book is dedicated to them. Lamentations is called Ekah ("how") in the Hebrew Bible. From its first word, how, the entire book is dedicated to deep mourning and ache. How much they had suffered, how much they grieved over their sin, how much they longed for God to bring restoration and how much they hoped in His rescue.

David

The melancholy author of Lamentations wasn't the only one who made use of "how." Another man in Scripture sang its refrain. In chapter 2, we surveyed the story of his great-grandmother and great-great-grandmother, Ruth and Naomi. We marveled at the hesed shown between them, imaging the redemptive nature of the Lord's steadfast love. Their progeny's name is David, one of the most notable people in the Bible. God refers to him as "a man after his own heart" (1 Sam. 13:14). The display of hesed continued to David even as he endured seasons of suffering the consequences of his own sin, or the pursuit of his demise by Saul (the king before him), or many other soul-wrenching times. The book of Psalms is filled with his laments in the midst of the desert but with the continued hope in God's *hesed*. Psalm 13 says:

How long, O LORD? Will you forget me forever?
How long will you hide your face from me?
How long must I take counsel in my soul
and have sorrow in my heart all the day?
How long shall my enemy be exalted over me?
Consider and answer me, O LORD my God;
light up my eyes, lest I sleep the sleep of death,
lest my enemy say, "I have prevailed over him,"
lest my foes rejoice because I am shaken.
But I have trusted in your steadfast love;
my heart shall rejoice in your salvation.
I will sing to the LORD,
because he has dealt bountifully with me.

The great "Prince of Preachers," C. H. Spurgeon, called this a howling psalm. Do you hear it? The longing? I am not surprised that a psalm—poetry meant to be sung—involves howling. My most frequent vocal accompanist is our Australian shepherd, Gus. When I scoot myself up to the piano and start lifting my voice in song, Gus rushes in to join me. His muzzle turns up, his eyes close, and he lets out a mournful note. He rarely lets me sing alone.

Canines use howling to communicate over long distances. It is fitting then, that the "how longs" are perceived as howls. David found himself far from the Lord. He verbalized the yearning with "how long will you hide your face from me?" Of this question in light of the other "how longs," Spurgeon writes:

This is a far more rational question, for God may hide his face, and yet he may remember still. A hidden face is no sign of a forgetful heart. It is in love that his face is turned away; yet to a real child of God, this hiding of his Father's face is terrible and he will never be at ease until, once more he hath his Father's smile.[1]

To howl, one must point her face up to the sky, to that which is above her. She, as David did, petitions the only One, though seemingly distant, who can do anything about her loneliness and longing. She searches the heavens to outline the faintest profile of her Father's countenance.

In Psalm 42, David accesses another animal analogy:

> *As a deer pants for flowing streams,*
> *so pants my soul for you, O God.*
> *My soul thirsts for God, for the living God.*
> *When shall I come and appear before God?*
> *My tears have been my food day and night,*
> *while they say to me all the day long,*
> *"Where is your God?" (vv. 1–3)*

How long? My soul pants for You, God! The longing in the desert isn't necessarily for evil things. Our desires may be right and good. It's not wrong for a deer to pant for the stream. In fact, it is by God's design that it does so for its own survival. And not just any stream but one that is flowing and fresh. Not like the glass of water on my nightstand that by morning's light tastes dusty. Our desire may be God Himself, the most refreshing stream, but even the right desire doesn't mean we don't feel hungry or thirsty or alone. The only nourishment we may find is in our own anemic tears.

And the mocking: "Where is your God?" Of course the enemy would show up at this hour. That's so him to make an appearance in the desert, to kick us when we're down. His derision doesn't just happen once. All day long, it says. He never takes a break.

DESERT SEASONS

I've had my share of howling and panting in the desert, and I'm only three and a half decades in. Two desert seasons I can recall with clarity. The first occurred early in our marriage. I was finishing up my last semester of college and Matt was in the thick of ministry. We called him the utility back on staff at church. His main charge was over the college ministry but he would also teach children's church, fill in the pulpit while our pastor was away, and even help compose by-laws. All of this was in addition to his position as Bible teacher at the large, collegiate, weekly gathering in town and as a traveling preacher.

Matt's calling was clear: preach the gospel and lead people. Everywhere I turned I saw confirmation. Whatever he found to do, it flourished. The Bible study grew from a few hundred to over a thousand. The college ministry thrived and multiplied. On staff, he was being groomed to eventually be a pastor himself or a ministry leader. Congregants regularly shared stories of the Lord using Matt to bring their friends and family to Christ or a breakthrough in their own relationship with the Lord.

From all appearances, Matt might as well have been chugging from the canteen while I watched with a sandy stare. Don't get me wrong, I was thrilled Matt was enjoying fruitfulness and drinking deeply from the well God provided. Being his wife, I got to appreciate the benefits. But only so far.

What about me, God? I'm here too!

Contentment eluded me. I was doing everything I was supposed to be doing. I dove into the life of our church. I served in the youth ministry. I discipled younger women. I went to class and made good grades. I sang on the worship team at the college Bible study.

Oh, that last one.

That's where I wanted to be fulfilled most. And that's where I felt the driest, the loneliest, the least fulfilled. The tension was strange. I struggled when I sang because I didn't like what I heard. I didn't feel as though I was offering my best. I didn't feel good enough. But I also struggled when I didn't sing. My pride was hurt when I wasn't invited to sing with the worship band. I felt an unceasing pull toward using my voice.

At one point I was so exasperated that I said to God, "If it's going to be this way, I'd rather You just take this desire from me completely!"

A little oasis in the desert came when He responded. Through someone I didn't know nor who knew little to nothing about me, God assured me that He had a purpose in this struggle and in using my voice to bring Him glory. I didn't realize it was only an oasis until I found myself wandering again through the sand and sun. He eventually led me out, but I'm saving that story for a later chapter.

The second jaunt in the desert was as recent as a few months ago. There wasn't a singular desire unfulfilled; it was more a whole season marked by drought. To sum it up in a word: numb. Things that once brought me joy and delight were barely a blip on my radar. I walked through life like a zombie, driven by the most basic instincts: eat, sleep, repeat.

I had committed to teaching at a women's conference in town, and I was regretting that decision something fierce. What did I have to offer? I was a mannequin, having a semblance of life but with nothing truly alive inside. But that was the problem. I was looking inward where there was only desert. I needed to look outward to the Source of refreshment. I pressed myself as hard as I could into the Lord. I found Him there. In my desiccation, He became a spring of water, a canteen, if you will.

Maybe you've felt this before, maybe you're right smack dab in the middle of it. Fellow sojourner, there's hope. Although the desert is daunting and you feel helplessly unable to find your way out, He is up to something. Take heart and hold on.

CHAPTER FOUR

The Way In

Some wandered in desert wastes,
finding no way to a city to dwell in;

Will you not judge me harshly if I share something that may come off a little boastful? I'm a pretty good driver. Navigating, driving defensively and proactively, I've got it down. Matt tells me that I've ruined him worse than Google Maps. If I'm riding shotgun, he completely forgets how to get anywhere. I'm a navigational crutch that keeps him from building his directional muscles. The cardinal points are my friends and they fail me rarely.

Sometimes though, my mind gets hijacked and I cruise into autopilot. I will step behind the wheel, mulling over an idea, a decision, a task, and wake up halfway to my destination without the slightest memory of the first leg of the trip. Yikes.

Maybe you've come to your senses and found yourself surrounded by a barren landscape asking yourself, "How on earth did I get here?"

Can you feel the heat? Is your soul weary? Are your cheeks windburned and stinging from the sand? Would it comfort you to just know how you got there? Because, if you knew how you got there, maybe you could retrace your steps toward home?

OUT OF EGYPT

The Israelites knew exactly how they found themselves in the desert. God led them there. Remember, God came to Moses, calling Himself "I AM WHO I AM," fueled by *hesed*, to lead His people out of Egypt. God didn't choose a direct route though. John Piper points out,

There are shorter ways to get from Egypt to Palestine than through the wilderness of Sinai. Mount Sinai is about 200 miles out of the way—which is bad enough if you are driving a car, but if you are walking and there is scarcely any water or shade, then the detour really tests your patience. You would think that if God were your travel agent, he would know the terrain and the shortest route to Palestine. You would think that if he can divide the Red Sea, a direct and painless route to the promised land would be a snap.[1]

The Lord is in the details. He doesn't charge ahead without thinking through and fully knowing every possible outcome with every possible step. God doesn't backtrack. Sure, He may lead you through familiar terrain but He's not retracing His steps because He forgot how He got you there. He is up to something. Because, He was up to something with the Israelites.

Though they had left Egypt, Egypt had not left them. They were still enslaved to the idols they had grown accustomed to there. They still trusted in the strength of the chariot, a roof over their head, and a future they could taste. Their slavery went deeper than their chains. They wanted what Egypt could provide more than they wanted what God promised. What Egypt held infinitely paled in comparison to what God offered.

God's people weren't supposed to stay in Egypt forever. If you'll think back, Joseph's brothers sought aid by sojourning to Egypt because of the famine in their land. God's *hesed* was shown through Joseph's kindness to his brothers despite their betrayal. He embraced them and provided for them.

Genesis 50:22 says that Joseph and his father's house remained in Egypt. But on his deathbed, Joseph reminded his brothers, "I am about to die, but God will visit you and bring you up out of this land to the land that he swore to Abraham, to Isaac, and to Jacob" (v. 24).

Joseph didn't want his family to forget the promise God had made to their forefathers. He didn't want them to mistake what God was providing temporarily for what He had for them permanently. It's as if Joseph took one of his brother's shoulders in his arthritic hands (belying the strength still left in them), squeezed him firmly, stared intently into his eyes and with his last breath said, "Don't forget this isn't our home."

My family tree is peppered with names like Schaffer and Huffman. The German limbs are stout and overshadowing. The qualities attributed to their ethic were unmistakable in my mother's childhood home. Her mother, Margie Schaffer, was German through and through. Her dark brown eyes could freeze lava when you slighted her but would warm to hot chocolate once an apology was made. Everything had a place in her house and she knew if something was awry. Cleanliness was most certainly next to godliness, especially when it came to one's teeth. A woman of German descent working in a dental office results in impeccable enamel and perfectly pale gums.

I loved going to Grandmother's. She made my favorite break-fast item: cheese toast with marshmallows on top. Don't scoff until you try it. The cheese is melted to perfection and the marshmallows brown just enough to encrust their gooey middles. Sweet and savory, and sticky. Needless to say, sugary snacks were never far from our reach. Neither was a toothbrush, floss, and a Waterpik with our very own personalized color attachment (mine was red). Every morning we were awakened with, "Good morning! Make sure you brush your teeth!" Every night we were warned, "Brush really well so the sugar doesn't eat holes in your pearly whites!"

The German genes were strong in Grandmother. She poked fun at her own German-ness, but she was always much more American than she was German. She had never seen its countryside, breathed its air, felt its pavement under her feet. But she could tell you exactly how to extract sap from an East Texas sweet gum tree and chew to your heart's content, or what color the hydrangeas would present in the acidic soil filling the beds behind her house. Texas was all the home she knew.

So it was with the descendants of Joseph and his brothers, those who God delivered through Moses, those who wandered in the wilderness. For four hundred thirty years, they and their pre-decessors knew nothing but Egypt as home. They only knew the azure sky that dropped behind the mud brick and mortar homes lining the dusty streets. They only knew the small, quiet life they eked out as slaves. Longing for freedom, their minds still couldn't grasp a reality without a taskmaster and Pharaoh's oppressive eye. The Promised Land seemed to them as attainable as a paid vacation.

The Lord loved them too much to leave them in delusion. The wilderness, or desert, was designed to bring them to their senses. To free them, body and soul, from Egypt.

"But it is because the LORD loves you and is keeping the oath that he swore to your fathers, that the LORD has brought you out with a mighty hand and redeemed you from the house of slavery, from the hand of Pharaoh king of Egypt" (Deut. 7:8).

The way through the wilderness may have felt like a detour but no more so than a trip to the doctor. When I wandered through my own desert season (the first I referred to in the previous chapter), I didn't know how sick I was until I felt the heat of my own feverish famine and suffered the dehydration of my false anchors. I had trusted in my own talents to set me apart, to make me feel good enough, desirable. Although with my lips I said I trusted the Lord to be enough for me, I was busy digging my own wells.

BROKEN WELLS

Insufficient wells are not a new thing. In Jeremiah 2:13 God brings this accusation against His people, "for my people have committed two evils: they have forsaken me, the fountain of living waters, and hewed out cisterns for themselves, broken cisterns that can hold no water."

John 4 recounts the interaction between Jesus and a woman with her own broken cisterns. Not coincidentally, it took place at a well. Jesus, weary from journeying, sat down for rest and refreshment. His rest and refreshment had less to do with relaxing and more to do with His relentless pursuit of doing the Father's work.

He saw her coming from a distance, her water jar balanced on her head. She looked toward the well with dashed hope. All she wanted was to draw the water in peace and quiet. That's why she chose the middle of the day. The women came in the cool of the morning, and their words burned more than the noonday sun.

Of all people, she may have seethed quietly, *a rabbi?*

I imagine she soothed herself with the thought that He would more than likely keep a distance and treat her as if she didn't exist. *That's what all the rabbis before had done.*

"Give me a drink."

His words startled her. Before she could stop her own, her thoughts took voice and revealed her astonishment.

"How is it that you, a Jew, ask for a drink from me, a woman of Samaria?" (John 4:9).

Samaritans were considered to be half-breeds. Their Jewish ancestors had "inter-married with Gentiles six centuries earlier and now followed their own version of Old Testament religion."[2] Most Jews avoided Samaritans at all cost. For Jesus, not only clearly Jewish but also clearly a teacher of the Law, to interact with this woman was beyond unusual. It would have been viewed as contaminating.

Jesus answered her, "If you knew the gift of God, and who it is that is saying to you, 'Give me a drink,' you would have asked him, and he would have given you living water" (v. 10).

This statement, to our modern ears, would have sounded arrogant. Maybe it sounded arrogant to this woman. If you knew who *I* was, *you* would have asked *Me*. But it's not arrogant; it's the truth. And arrogance would have this woman serving Him, but He suggested that He would serve her. How is this possible?

"For even the Son of Man came not to be served but to serve, and to give his life as a ransom for many" (Mark 10:45). Jesus came to expose our thirst and to reveal God as the only fountain that will ever satisfy.

The woman was still confused by His statement, though.

"Sir, you have nothing to draw water with, and the well is deep. Where do you get that living water? Are you greater than our father Jacob? He gave us the well and drank from it himself, as did his sons and his livestock."

Jesus said to her, "Everyone who drinks of this water will be thirsty again, but whoever drinks of the water that I will give him will never be thirsty again. The water that I will give him will become in him a spring of water welling up to eternal life." (John 4:11–14)

This sounded like just what this woman needed. No more midday trips to the well. No more aching muscles from carrying the jar back and forth day after day. No more chance encounters with mysterious rabbis. No more thirst.

The woman said to him, "Sir, give me this water, so that I will not be thirsty or have to come here to draw water" (v. 15).

This is where Jesus "kept it real."

"Go, call your husband, and come here" (v. 16).

This statement cut the woman to the quick. If there was one thing she had hoped to hide, it was this, the topic of every whisper when the women of the village drew water with her.

"I have no husband" (v. 17).

Jesus said to her, "You are right in saying, 'I have no husband'; for you have had five husbands, and the one you now have is not your husband. What you have said is true" (vv. 17–18).

God doesn't pull punches. He sees right through our veneer to the heart and goes for it. This was a little too close for comfort for the woman. I've found myself in the same posture—defensively deflective.

"Sir, I perceive that you are a prophet. Our fathers worshiped on this mountain, but you say that in Jerusalem is the place where people ought to worship" (vv. 19–20).

The woman shifted from the personal to the theological without realizing that the theological is personal. What we believe about God and who He is, and what we believe about ourselves in light of that is revealed in our most personal places. The Samaritan woman's theology was exposed by where she got her thirst quenched.

"Woman, believe me, the hour is coming when neither on this mountain nor in Jerusalem will you worship the Father. You worship what you do not know; we worship what we know, for salvation is from the Jews. But the hour is coming, and is now here, when the true worshipers will worship the Father in spirit and truth, for the Father is seeking such people to worship him. God is spirit, and those who worship him must worship in spirit and truth" (vv. 21–24).

Jesus didn't pat her on the head and say, "Don't worry your pretty little head about such things." He also didn't skirt the issue of her ethnic background. He met her question and thirst head-on. He boiled it down to this: it's not the where of worship; it's the how (in Spirit and truth) and Whom of worship.

The woman said to him, "I know that Messiah is coming (he who is called Christ). When he comes, he will tell us all things."

Jesus said to her, "I who speak to you am he" (vv. 25–26).

No one is too small in God's eyes. No one's thirst is too insignificant to Him. Jesus revealed Himself to a woman who didn't receive a religious person's time of day. He made known to her His identity and the truth behind her desire to be filled.

So the woman left her water jar and went away into town and said to the people, "Come, see a man who told me all that I ever did. Can this be the Christ?" (v. 28–29).

She left her water jar. It no longer enslaved her. That heavy, half-the-time empty vessel was abandoned at the well. Jesus met her at her well. He pointed out her thirst and poured out His sufficiency to satisfy it.

It's okay to be thirsty. God gives us thirst. It's where we satisfy our thirst that matters.

For the woman, God used a providential encounter at her well to unmask her thirst and make known the Source that will never run dry. For the Israelites, God used the desert to diagnose their thirst and expose the deficiency of Egypt's ability to quench it. You may find yourself in the desert because God loved you too much to let you live as a slave to your own Egypt and your own wells. He has drawn you into the wilderness because of His lovingkindness to expose Egypt and the wells for what they are—false anchors. What do you receive in return? Freedom.

BETRAYAL AND FIDELITY

When God calls us to do something, we usually assume it will be honorable and respectable. Most of the time, if not always, it is. However, what's honorable in His eyes may be different from what we understand.

The Old Testament includes the story of Hosea, a man God chose for a scandalous calling—to take a prostitute as his wife. Gomer wasn't recovering from her trade; she was right in the middle of participating in it.

The Lord did not lead Hosea astray in this. He was painting a picture for His people in shockingly vivid colors. He was exhibiting how serious He was in arresting His people's affections and how passionate He was in securing their fidelity and joy.

Israel was experiencing one of its most turbulent time periods. In only thirty years, they were ruled by six different kings. Almost every ruler met a disastrous fate; most were assassinated or murdered by neighboring regimes. To say the least, these were unsettling times. The chaotic atmosphere wasn't relegated to the leadership but found its roots in the constituency.

Worship of Baal ran rampant through the nation. Baal was the Syrian-Palestinian god of weather. He was attributed with power over agriculture, rainfall, productivity, and fertility. As an agricultural society, the temptation to "cover one's bases" was strong.

Yeah, *"the Lord our God, the Lord is one."*

But just in case that's not the case, a little hazard insurance paid directly to Baal wouldn't hurt, right?

The currency was sex. The place of business, the shrine. "Sexual behavior at these shrines was expected to cause the Baals to respond in like manner—to follow the worshipers by producing for them fertile seed and rain for a good crop."[3] The worshipers entered into sexual acts with cult prostitutes. Gomer, Hosea's wife, was among their number. She represented Israel's idolatry. Her adultery mirrored theirs.

"For she said, 'I will go after my lovers,
who give me my bread and my water,
my wool and my flax, my oil and my drink.'
Therefore I will hedge up her way with thorns,
and I will build a wall against her,
so that she cannot find her paths.
She shall pursue her lovers but not overtake them,
and she shall seek them but shall not find them.

Then she shall say,
'I will go and return to my first husband,
for it was better for me then than now.'
And she did not know
that it was I who gave her
the grain, the wine, and the oil,
and who lavished on her silver and gold,
which they used for Baal." (Hosea 2:5-8)

As Gomer had betrayed Hosea, so had Israel betrayed their God. They had given themselves to other lovers and forsaken their Husband. The Lord's taking them to be His own wasn't about keeping rules. It wasn't about an exchange of services. He didn't require their worship and obedience so that they could get what they really wanted: plentiful crops and overflowing quivers. In fact, although Israel attributed their accumulation of grain, wine, oil, silver, and gold to their idols, it was God who lavished these on them even in the midst of their betrayal.

The *hesed* vow is not transactional; it is deeply relational. The covenant made between God and His people is like a marriage, not a business arrangement. He is a deeply jealous God. Not in a creepy, stalker way, but in a loving, husband way.

Imagine there's a married woman who works in an office. Day in and day out, she meets with clients and coworkers, developing ideas and relationships. In her office is a man who happens to swing by her door every morning. Over a period of time she notices he starts dropping by more often throughout the day. Eventually, he starts walking her to her car every evening. She is flattered by his presence but unsure of his intentions until one evening he makes them clear. She is appalled by his behavior and frustrated at herself for not seeing it sooner. Her drive home is filled with anxiety over how her husband will react. She walks through the door, her shoulders heavy with angst, and unloads the story to her husband. He listens intently and nods with concern.

What if he looked at her and said, "Well, if you like him, go for it"? Do you think she would feel especially loved? I know I'd be thinking, *What is he up to that he's okay with this?* This is not the kind of response one would want to hear from one's spouse!

I know what Matt would say. First, he would be hurt that I entertained this man's attention for so long. Second, he would want that man's name, cell number, home address, and license plate number. He would hunt the man down and let him know (in so many words) that his affection toward me is not welcome. Now, that's the kind of jealous that makes a girl feel loved. That's the kind of jealous God is for our worship. He doesn't sit idly by and say, "Oh well, if it works for you." With ferocity, He goes after our hearts by crushing our idols and hedging up our way to them. He draws us into a desert to lay our false anchors to waste for our good and His glory.

> "Therefore, behold, I will allure her,
> and bring her into the wilderness,
> and speak tenderly to her.
> And there I will give her her vineyards
> and make the Valley of Achor a door of hope.
> And there she shall answer as in the days of her youth,
> as at the time when she came out of the land of Egypt.
> And in that day, declares the LORD, you will call me 'My Husband,' and no longer will you call me 'My Baal.' For I will remove the names of the Baals from her mouth, and they shall be remembered by name no more. And I will make for them a covenant on that day with the beasts of the field, the birds

*of the heavens, and the creeping things of the ground. And I
will abolish the bow, the sword, and war from the land, and I
will make you lie down in safety. And I will betroth you to me
forever. I will betroth you to me in righteousness and in justice,
in steadfast love and in mercy. I will betroth you to me in
faithfulness. And you shall know the LORD." (Hosea 2:14–20)*

God loves His people too much to let them continue on in their
idolatry. He will go to extremes to free them. In Hosea, He drew
them into the wilderness so they would exchange their transactional notion of worship for the relational and forsake their adul-
terous affair with idols and be found faithful to their Husband.

The Lord has lovingly uncovered my Gomer-heart and hedged
up my way to other lovers. In the middle of it, I was devastated. I
felt like God was holding out on me. I thought to myself, *If He loved
me, He would let me have this.* I got one thing right: He loved me.
He loved me enough to entice me into the wilderness so that He
could remove the "Baals" from my mouth—that I would no longer
call on them for significance and meaning. He bound my heart to
His and promised to remain faithful even when I would fall into
faithlessness (2 Tim. 2:13).

Perhaps you can identify with me. Maybe there's a part of you
that feels neglected by the Lord. If He would just come through
with this one thing, you'd know He loves you. What if receiving
that one thing would tighten your grip on the idol instead of stirring your heart toward the Lord? I don't ask this in a vacuum. I
know what it's like to have God say, "No"—to have Him remove an
idol in my heart. I also know the freedom that comes from finding
all I ever need in Him.

SUFFERING AND FRUITFULNESS

God often leads His people into the desert in order to free them from their ties to idols and broken wells, and to betroth them to Himself in faithfulness. Sometimes, though, He leads them to the desert not just for sanctification but also for preparation. Christ was on the cusp of His earthly ministry when His loving Father took Him into the desert. The road ahead would be fraught with difficulty and trepidation, but it would yield immeasurable fruit.

Scripture states that Jesus, God in the flesh, "was led by the Spirit in the wilderness for forty days, being tempted by the devil" (Luke 4:1–2). While He was in the wilderness, He ate nothing. He was stripped of everything that would bring comfort except for the presence of the Holy Spirit. He knew what it was like to be hungry and thirsty, tired and uncomfortable.

Right on cue, Satan showed up.

"If you are the Son of God, command this stone to become bread" (v. 3).

The enemy called Jesus' identity into question and appealed to His instinctive desire for food. He wanted Jesus to doubt His true identity and cave to entitlement. As I've pointed out before, Satan has no new tricks. He held out forbidden fruit to Jesus, but this time it was bread. And unlike Adam and Eve, Jesus remained firm in who He is and resisted presumption.

"It is written, 'Man shall not live by bread alone'" (v. 4).

And the devil took him up and showed him all the kingdoms of the world in a moment of time, and said to him, "To you I will give all this authority and their glory, for it has been delivered to me, and I give it to whom I will. If you, then, will worship me, it will all be yours" (vv. 6–7).

Whose glory would Jesus be about? Would He abuse His power and position for personal gain or would He remain faithful to the task? Would He make a deal with the devil or preserve His perfect obedience?

Of course, the blameless Son of God responded, "It is written, 'You shall worship the Lord your God, and him only shall you serve'" (v. 8).

Satan made one more attempt to trip up the Savior. He recited a twisted version of Scripture to hook Him. Taking Him up to the pinnacle of the temple in Jerusalem, he said, "If you are the Son of God, throw yourself down from here, for it is written, 'He will command his angels concerning you, to guard you,' and 'On their hands they will bear you up, lest you strike your foot against a stone'" (vv. 9–11).

The Word made flesh was not thrown for a loop. He saw through the enemy's scheme. He used Scripture to interpret Scripture.

"It is said, 'You shall not put the Lord your God to the test'" (v. 12).

The record of His temptation shows us a few things. It shows us how God might use temptation (although He is never the author of it) to further root our identity in Him, uproot entitlement, strengthen our desire to be about His glory, and burn Scripture into our hearts for the impending season. If you're in the midst of a desert, be looking for these evidences of God's work in your life. Be encouraged that He might be leading you through a time of suffering or wilderness so that you may bear much fruit in a time of ministry.

This account also proves that Jesus is doing something new and better. Where Adam and Eve failed their temptation, Jesus prevailed. In all the ways Eve responded to the serpent miserably, Jesus answered resolutely. He is the true and better Adam.[4]

Last, we can be encouraged that when we inevitably give in to the temptations that come our way, there was One who did not.

We can claim His righteousness as our own because we know we have none apart from Him.

HE GOES WITH US

It's a comfort to know that in the middle of our desert we're not alone. In each scenario I've put before you, God was there. His presence went with the Israelites as they left Egypt. Jesus sat with the soul-thirsty woman at the well. The Lord drew His Gomer-hearted people into the desert to show His fidelity despite their infidelity. Jesus was full of the Spirit and led by the Spirit in the wilderness.

He didn't shove them along and say, "Good luck getting to the other side!"

He went with them.

And He goes with us.

He may seem far, but if you are His, if you are a child of God, He is close. Draw near to Him; He has promised to draw near to you (James 4:8). He is working something in the desert—plucking false anchors, filling wells, tilling the soil of our hearts to receive seeds to bear fruit. Let Him do His work but do not neglect to cry for His help. We aren't meant for the desert forever. He has a way out.

CHAPTER FIVE

The Way Out

He led them by a straight way
till they reached a city to dwell in.

My parents weren't due to be home for another hour, plenty of time to whip up a cake. What's that you say? Instructions? Nah, I'm good. A few scoops of flour here, a dash of sugar there. A little bit of salt and whatever's in this small orange box in the fridge for good measure. Gotta make it wet somehow. I know, water! Stir with a whisk, pour into a pan, bake at 350 degrees for, I don't know, I'll just keep an eye on it.

The odor, er, aroma, wafted in the air, filling the kitchen. It had only been twenty minutes but it must be ready! Hands tucked into mitts, eyes eager for a baked delight, I removed the cake from the oven. To call this thing "cake" was generous. To call it edible was delusional.

For a hardly domesticated twelve-year-old, improvisational baking was a stretch. I had watched my mom bake melt-in-your-mouth pound cakes and throw together her own scrumptious versions of culinary staples, but I had yet to learn the art of following a recipe. Adhering to my instincts and striking out on my own produced terrible results. There are some things better to be done with help. Help from a well-tried, well-written method, or help from someone who knows what they're doing.

Finding one's own way out of the desert is like me finding my own way to bake a cake. You may not end up with a mouth full of bland mortar mix, but you will find yourself stuck. Psalm 107:4 says those who wandered in the desert found no way to a city to dwell in. This means they at least tried. They may have seen light from the cities in the distance but failed to discover a road in. So how did they manage to get out?

Then they cried to the Lord in their trouble,
and he delivered them from their distress. (Ps. 107:6)

They cried to the Lord. Not when they ceased feeling hungry, tired, thirsty, and hopeless, or when they managed to stiffen their upper lip and act like everything was fine, but right in the middle of their desert, right in the middle of their beaten-down sighing. Too often I feel as though I need to pull myself together in order to cry out to the Lord. If my circumstances aren't rosy, I can at least pretend I'll get through it somehow. That's not what we see here. They cried to Him *in their trouble.*

Why do I believe I have to be presentable? In a word: pride. I am too proud to admit that I'm at the end of my rope, that I wasn't smart enough to figure it out by myself. This is a dangerous place to be. Pride will keep us wandering in our wastelands and wildernesses.

James 4:6 tells us, "God opposes the proud, but gives grace to the humble." It takes humility to cry out to the Lord in our distress.

Our crying out proves that we can't do it alone. It exposes us for what we are: poor and needy.

POOR AND NEEDY

When you peruse the magazine rack at the local grocery store, rarely do you see an indigent "nobody" on the covers. According to marketing research, that sort of thing doesn't sell. What will sell is the rich and famous splashed on the front with air-brushed complexions and Photoshopped waistlines. Media holds up the rich and powerful and disdains the poor and needy. Before you point your finger at the media, we're the ones buying their wares. It's not glamorous to receive the handout; it's glamorous to be seen giving a handout. We'd rather picture ourselves with an apron wrapped around our waist, a ladle of soup perched above a homeless man's bowl, and our white teeth shining as paparazzi snaps a shot. But to be the man with the bowl? No thanks.

In God's economy, the poor and needy are the ones who have His attention and receive His help:

When the poor and needy seek water,
and there is none,
and their tongue is parched with thirst,
I the LORD will answer them;
the God of Israel will not forsake them.
I will open rivers on the bare heights,
and fountains in the midst of the valleys.
I will make the wilderness a pool of water,
and the dry land springs of water.
I will put in the wilderness the cedar,
the acacia, the myrtle, and the olive.

I will set in the desert the cypress,
the plane and the pine together,
that they may see and know,
may consider and understand together,
that the hand of the LORD *has done this,*
the Holy One of Israel has created it. (Isa. 41:17–20)

We see it again. God's people—the poor and needy, the humble—acknowledge their thirst and cry out to God in the midst of it. The Lord responds by bringing water from dry land and planting trees in the barren places. He gives them a spring for their thirst and shade from the heat. They receive the help, and He gets the glory. This is as it should be. We are the created, He, the Creator. We can celebrate a piece of art or music, but it's the artist that deserves the praise.

So in that paparazzi snapshot, we're the homeless man offering up his bowl to be filled, and God is the celebrity doling out the soup and shining in the spotlight. The difference is, we can know God's true intentions. The celebrity's motives may be altruistic or egocentric. We can't tell from the outside looking in, and he or she may not be able to untangle what's truly fueling the benevolence. But with God, we know He always acts in steadfast love for His children. It's who He is.

It's good to remember His nature—that He's good, loving, and all-knowing—because crying out involves confession. Admitting my sin to someone who I'm not sure likes me or much less loves me and wants good for me is a perilous position. Who knows what they might do with the information I entrust to them. But God is not only loving, He is the only one who will receive my confession and be able to offer cleansing and forgiveness (1 John 1:9). We must admit our poverty and need. We must be willing to look at the idols, broken wells, and shackles of Egypt still left in us. We must be willing to leave them behind. Or, if there's no blatant idolatry, we must admit our thirst—that we feel dry, alone, and know no other way out but Him.

HE LED THEM

Our oldest daughter, Audrey, has become a full-fledged horse girl. Most afternoons, she is either on the trail, in the arena, or racing barrels, but no matter what, she's on the back of her horse. Gypsy is a copper-colored quarter horse who's won her way into our hearts. I'm amazed every time I watch Audrey ride Gypsy. This girl who doesn't weigh 100 pounds soaking wet can maneuver her 800-pound horse with a rope tied on both ends to a small piece of metal in the horse's mouth. Even on more stubborn days, Gypsy only needs a swift nudge from a spur's edge to cooperate.

I'm not fooled though. There is a give and take happening. At any moment, Gypsy could downright refuse to be bossed around anymore and send Audrey flying in the air hitting the ground hard. It happened more often in our early days with her but is now a rare occurrence. Audrey has gained Gypsy's trust. She has been faithful to feed her, groom her, and tend to her hooves when a rock is lodged in her shoe. She's nursed her wounds and rewarded her for hard work. Audrey has nuzzled her head into the crook of Gypsy's neck and scratched her in just the right place that sends her head back and nose up in sheer pleasure.

Despite over a year of consistent love and care, Gypsy still shows signs of insecurity when she's put in a new situation. The latest scenario was when we tried to load her into a trailer. We had placed a halter on Gypsy to lead her. Usually with the halter, she follows with no problem, making you believe the rope is what's forcing her to move with you. The ruse was up when she stopped just short of the ramp. No amount of tugging on that rope made her budge. After an hour of much coaxing and even more tears, Gypsy loaded. Everyone broke into shouts and cries of relief. From then on, Audrey worked with her consistently, placing her feed in the bin inside the trailer. She proved to Gypsy that walking into the trailer was safe and good, and that she could trust Audrey to lead her.

Once we've come to the place where we admit we're poor and needy and have humbled ourselves to cry out to God, He will lead us out of the desert. To be led implies there's following involved—a yielding of one's will to another. It's nice when those wills line up naturally, but stretching when they don't. In Audrey and Gypsy's case, Gypsy will gladly submit to Audrey's direction when she's bringing her back to the barn after a long trail ride. Gypsy knows relief is coming and heartily yields. When it comes to something new like the trailer, she's timid, unwilling, and an abundance of assurance is required for her obedience.

Are we not unlike Gypsy? We're all in if the path seems pleasurable but the moment things get hard or the way is unfamiliar, we dig our heels (or hooves) into the sand and refuse to budge. Oh, but if we would trust Him to lead us all the way. If we would yield our wills to Him and know Him more deeply on the journey back to "a city to dwell in," knowing that relief is coming if we trust Him.

A STRAIGHT WAY

The way back is described as being "straight." When the Israelites wandered in the desert after their escape from Egypt, their winding way was a result of God's dealing with the idols still left in their hearts and their refusal to trust Him for the Promised Land. He was squeezing what was left of Egypt out of them. They walked right up to the edge, spied giants in the land, and didn't believe the same God who delivered them from the Egyptians could overcome the giants. For forty years they wandered in the wilderness until Moses died and God appointed Joshua to "arise, go over this Jordan, you and all this people, into the land that I am giving them, to the people of Israel" (Josh. 1:2).

It was that simple. Arise and go because I, the Lord, am going with you. And they did. And it wasn't easy. Straight doesn't mean easy, but we can definitely make it more challenging. Hebrews 12:13 tells us to make straight paths for our feet, "so that what is lame may not be put out of joint but rather be healed." In other words, don't dig potholes for yourself. Wear the appropriate shoes and get moving.

For a season, my friend and I faithfully ran multiple miles together. I have grown to love running, but it took having friends by my side to get there. To protect her identity, this friend will remain nameless. You'll soon understand why.

Our favorite time to run was at night after kids were put to bed. We felt like we weren't stealing time from our children and leaving our husbands to wrangle them into their beds alone. The problem with running at night is that not all paths were well lit, and my friend has a penchant for tripping.

On one run, we were chatting away when suddenly my friend was no longer in sight. I looked to the space beside me where she had been seconds before and she was gone! I stopped in my tracks and turned around. She was laid out in the grass giggling uncontrollably, her palms raw and knee bleeding.

"What happened?!?"

"I tripped over something and couldn't keep myself from falling!"

She and I inspected the sidewalk behind us. On the side where she had been running was a narrow manhole that protruded several inches above the concrete. Someone was having a bad day when they put that in.

We thought we had solved the problem when we decided to run one sunny afternoon. Not so much. The sidewalk had run out along our way so we ran on the shoulder of the road against traffic. The street was very lightly traveled apart from a few cars. As one approached, we adjusted accordingly and hugged the side. We didn't think through who was dangerously close to the ditch. And of course, my friend's foot failed to adjust to the sloped terrain and she fell headlong into a pile of leaves. We have decided that maybe walking or running on a treadmill would be best for us—at least for her sake. On second thought, a treadmill may be a little too much. Walking it is!

We tried to make straight paths for our feet. We adjusted our routes and times to set my friend up for the best outcome. She and I did what we could to avoid dimly lit sidewalks, protruding manholes, and narrow shoulders. Likewise, Scripture implores us to do what we can to make straight paths for our feet. As we exit the desert, it's helpful to identify any potholes (or manholes) along our way. What do I mean by this? There are some things that aren't sinful in and of themselves but serve as distractions. We can be distracted from God's leading us out of the desert and thus slow down the process. Too much television and time on social media keeps me focused on the temporary instead of digging deep into His Word. I'm not saying television, Twitter, and Facebook are evil, but I can find myself honing in on what to remodel in my house, what kind of boots to wear now, where someone has been invited to go (and, humph, I haven't!), what such-and-such has to say about this Scripture, what's the latest cause to undertake, and on and on it goes. They are potholes that slow my exit out of the desert. When I'm willing to resist the temptation to "just check quickly" what's going on in the digital world, I find my heart is more at peace and primed to meet with the Lord and be led by His Word.

IT'S A JOURNEY

Matt travels internationally roughly twice a year. He tries not to go too often because he's somewhat of a homebody. Around the fifth day of his trip, he can usually be found misty-eyed, listening to sappy country music, and scrolling through pictures of our family. It's quite sad, really. Praise God for technology, in particular, iChat. When photos aren't enough, Matt logs into the video-messaging app and there we appear in the (digitalized) flesh. As the trip comes to an end, it never fails that he laments the fact that no one has yet to come up with the teleporter. You know, the device that Captain Kirk used to "beam me up, Scotty." There's at least one long plane ride, if not more, in his future before he walks through our front door. When he boards that jet, he knows he still has hours until he reaches home, but he's comforted by the fact that he's at least one step closer.

The straight way out of the desert is a journey. Although Jesus seems to be able to travel teleporter style (Luke 24:31), the Lord generally works within the bounds of time and space with us. Endurance is something He values and it's something He does well. In Romans 15:5, He is called the "God of endurance." He displays His patient endurance with us as He does not quickly send His Son back but tarries so that many would have the opportunity to repent and turn to Him in faith (2 Pet. 3:9). We are encouraged to run with endurance the race that is set before us (Heb. 12:1). Endurance is a quality that builds character and hope (Rom. 5:4). In Revelation, Jesus commends those who exhibit patient endurance (Rev. 2:2, 19; 3:10). Since Scripture clearly indicates God prizes endurance, we can expect He will build it in us as we journey with Him.

A CITY TO DWELL IN

Be encouraged that the journey isn't aimless; there is a destination. He leads His people to a city to dwell in. Spurgeon puts it beautifully, "The end was worthy of the way: he did not lead them from one desert to another, but he gave the wanderers an abode, the weary ones a place of rest."[1] The city is everything the desert isn't: protection, rest, and community.

Ancient cities were surrounded by great walls. These provided protection for the citizens against intruders. We can be assured that when the Lord brings us to a city to dwell in, we will find refuge therein. With refuge comes rest.

During the first few months of Norah's life, she would wake in the early hours of the morning, as all infants do, hungry. As I fed her in the living room, away from the rest of the sleeping family, I would watch a program on television called *Survivorman*. Basically, the show is about a man being dropped in the middle of nowhere with little to no food, water, a camera, and not much else, and he has to survive for seven to ten days on his own. Depending on his location, he uses different techniques for survival. Usually it's a method borrowed from the natives who originally occupied the land. Once though, he kept a fire going with a Frito. That's how much oil saturates the corn chip; essentially, when you eat a Frito, you're consuming a tasty candle.

The first order of business, wherever he was abandoned, was to find shelter and start a fire. For forty-four minutes, I watched him build a shelter, start and keep a fire, find food, and try (and usually fail) to sleep. At the time, I wasn't sure why I was so drawn to this show. As I look back, though, I think I commiserated with him in his lack of sleep. My bleary-eyed self subconsciously found solace in his miserable plight to sleep! However, I'll choose my lot of sleeplessness over his any time. My insomnia was due to a sweet little baby; his was due to less than safe circumstances. Animals lurked in the darkness, insects invaded every inch of personal space, and in one episode, Survivorman made his shelter in a narrow cleft of a cliff. Although he placed what he could on the outer edge to keep himself from rolling to his death, sleep evaded him. No matter where he made his bed, he was never completely secure, and thus could not completely rest.

Rest

God is serious about rest. He listed it among the Ten Commandments, "Remember the Sabbath day, to keep it holy" (Exod. 20:8). He modeled rest for us when He created the universe (Gen. 2:2–3). No part of Him needed the rest, but He knew we would need it.

God could have created us like the Energizer Bunny. We could just keep going and going. But He didn't. Since nothing He does is without meaning, there must be something happening here. There's something He wants to show us.

The Sabbath was created as a time to pause from the normal routine—a time to cease going about our own business and focus on what God has done for us. To observe the Sabbath is an act of trust. The Lord's people must trust Him to sustain and provide for their needs. When Moses and the Israelites were wandering the desert, God provided heavenly manna for them to eat (Exod. 16:14–31). Every day they were instructed to gather only what they needed for that day. Anything left over was to be thrown out or else it would breed worms and stink. But on the sixth day, they were to gather enough for two days so that they could fully rest on the Sabbath. Miraculously, the residual portion was free of worms and stench. The Lord gave them exactly what they needed and preserved a portion for them.

We can trust God to provide when we rest. Resting is trusting in action. Each night we have the opportunity to practice resting: we sleep! "The benefits of sleep are obvious. As we sleep, strength is restored, the mind is cleared, and we're prepared to serve God another day . . . God could have created us without a need for sleep . . . Each night, as I confront my need again for sleep, I'm reminded that I'm a dependent creature. I am not self-sufficient. I am not the Creator. There is only One who 'will neither slumber nor sleep' (Ps. 121:4), and I am not that One."[2]

Walls

We can observe the Sabbath and practice resting by sleeping, but what does this really look like? The heart of the Sabbath is to cease striving and trust God's work on our behalf. The walls of "the city to dwell in" are wrought by God. Too many times I have attempted to build my own walls of protection and thus manufacture my own rest. Like that tasteless cake, I throw random ingredients together, hoping for a favorable outcome. The shopping list:

A regular "quiet time."
Church attendance.
Leading a Bible study.
Discipling younger women.
Parenting my children with patience and self-control.
Keeping my home in order.
Pleasing my husband.
Serving the least.
Giving my time and money.
Writing something noteworthy.
Instagramming a perfectly appointed moment.
Knowing that people like me.

I mix them together. Stir well. Wipe the sweat out of my eyes. Bake them in a 350-degree oven. And they melt under the heat. Another ineffective anchor. The walls come tumbling down because I can't even bake a simple brick.

I attend church but my mind is distracted by my to-do list.

Stamina wanes halfway through a 12-week Bible study.

The enthusiasm I had at the beginning of the mentoring relationship fizzles.

I lose it with my kids.

The laundry piles high. Dust bunnies stage a coup.

Sleep tempts me to stay "five more minutes" in bed instead of five more minutes in His Word.

Matt and I are just "off."

My schedule fills with serving only those who can reciprocate.

Sometimes I just want to browse TJ Maxx for stuff I don't need.

The cursor blinks a blank stare. My words fall flat.

My Instagrammable moment is eclipsed by the next person's.

Someone tweets a nasty, judgmental phrase about me.

My walls don't hold. The Lord is my only enduring stronghold. With all honesty, I can claim King David's words in Psalm 27,

> The LORD is my light and my salvation;
> whom shall I fear?
> The LORD is the stronghold of my life;
> of whom shall I be afraid?
> When evildoers assail me
> to eat up my flesh,
> my adversaries and foes,
> it is they who stumble and fall.
> Though an army encamp against me,
> my heart shall not fear;
> though war arise against me,
> yet I will be confident. (Ps. 27:1–3)

All the effort to protect myself isn't enough. The walls God provides were built with blood, sweat, and tears. But not mine. Praise God. They belong to Jesus. His life and death cover my sins—my failed attempts to provide refuge and relief. I can find rest in Jesus' work for me. This rest isn't just for me but for anyone who would believe in Him, anyone who would throw up their hands in surrender saying, "I can't, but I believe You, Jesus, already did."

Community

Not only did Jesus' life on earth and death on the cross bring refuge and rest, He purchased a people for God. The city is brimming with people from all backgrounds. There is no "type" except those who have faith to believe. No longer are we alone. We have fellowship with one another.

My friend Lisa and her daughter, Gracie, had gone through a rough year. They moved out of a living arrangement that had become toxic. Although they were grateful to escape, their leaving was with much pain and sorrow. Being on their own wasn't as wonderful as they'd hoped it would be. Lisa, in particular, felt alone. Then she met Pam.

Pam extended a lifeline to them—a place to live and community. She invited Lisa and Gracie to our church. They sat almost every Sunday morning for months beside Pam and her family, listening to Matt's sermons and singing songs to the Lord. Lisa grew up knowing about God, but He had yet to become real to her.

We met Lisa through a mutual friend. Audrey had been taking horseback riding lessons from this friend, but she thought Lisa would be a better fit. She had the time and space to devote attention to Audrey's development as a rider. She knew we needed Lisa, and Lisa might need us. At that time I couldn't have imagined how much.

Audrey was spending large amounts of time with Lisa and becoming her protégé. She wanted boots like Lisa. She wore the same kind of shirts and jeans as Lisa. She drank too much Pepsi like Lisa. We wanted to know who Lisa was—what was she really like? We opened our hearts and home to her and Gracie. Over the past two years they have become family. Lisa came to a saving knowledge of Christ. I got to stand with her in front of our church as she testified to God's faithfulness toward her. I've watched her struggle well, pore over God's Word, and be surrounded by people who love her. Pam's and our family are not the only ones. Many from The Village have wrapped their hearts around Lisa and Gracie. Once alone and on her own, now she belongs to a community who made God tangible.

Real, loving, biblical community does that. It puts flesh on the unseen. Men and women become the hands and feet of God. They sit across from us, look us in the eye, place a hand on our shoulder. They listen as we pour out our hearts. They pray with us. They pray for us when our words struggle to surface. They preach the gospel to us when we forget what it sounds like. They point us to Scripture and remind us of the Truth.

For those of us who live in this "city to dwell in," we've all been led out of the desert of unbelief and into fellowship with God and His people through faith in Christ. We know what it's like to wander and be warmly received. We remember the brass heavens, the mouthful of sand, the sighing, the lamenting. Though our deserts may have looked vastly different, we have been delivered by the same Lord with the same steadfast love.

> Let them thank the LORD for his steadfast love,
> for his wondrous works to the children of man!
> For he satisfies the longing soul,
> and the hungry soul he fills with good things. (Ps. 107:8–9)

PART THREE

Chains

(PSALM 107:10–16)

Some sat in darkness and in the shadow of death,
prisoners in affliction and in irons,
for they had rebelled against the words of God,
and spurned the counsel of the Most High.
So he bowed their hearts down with hard labor;
they fell down, with none to help.
Then they cried to the Lord *in their trouble,*
and he delivered them from their distress.
He brought them out of darkness and the shadow of death,
and burst their bonds apart.
Let them thank the Lord *for his steadfast love,*
for his wondrous works to the children of man!
For he shatters the doors of bronze
and cuts in two the bars of iron.

⚓

CHAPTER SIX

Heavy

The restrained cries squeezed barbed-wire in my throat. A man on the stage with whom I'd shared barely a sentence must have read my mail. He talked about a field and the owner who wanted to cultivate it. But for the weeds, nothing would grow. At first he tried mowing it—lopping the leggy tops and unsightly leaves. For a while it feigned lovely but an afternoon rain washed away the charade. The tops and leaves sprouted to new heights. The owner, though dismayed, was undeterred. He dropped knee to dirt, hands to plant, and pulled with all his might. He arose victorious with weed in hand. Another afternoon rain and a few days' sunshine revealed his work was not enough. Although the plants had been removed, their roots still clung to the earth. He just couldn't do it on his own. Something greater, stronger had to do it for him.

I knew he was talking about me. I had tried so hard to get it right. To be the good girl. To earn favor with God and man. But I failed, and miserably so. I was right there in the dirt with the land-owner—mud under my nails, grass-stained knees, aching bones. Every time I'd think I had a hold of my temper or jealousy or envy, a sprout pushed through the dirt.

My eyes desperately followed the man as he paced before us describing the field, the landowner, and his predicament. I swallowed hard but the barbs dug deeper. I was so weary. Was I finally weary enough?

The teacher closed in prayer and extended an invitation to those whose hearts had been pricked by the message—anyone willing to surrender the mowing and the digging. A man and a woman stood in front of him ready to receive anyone who would come. One by one, people from all over the room stood and made their way to the front. I watched as they were embraced, tears and all. Each was given a blue poker chip with something inscribed on both sides. I wondered what it said. Even more so, I wondered what it felt like to hold it in my own hand. To admit weakness and imperfection. To be brave enough to stand. I sat among these people as their pastor's wife. What would they think of me?

The service moved on to the next segment. I had missed it. I wouldn't know what the writing said or what freedom felt like. Again the barbs dug deeper. My eyes burned with regret. The teacher's voice interrupted the internal verbal lashing I was giving myself. Once more, he said, they would offer the chance to come forth and receive a hug and that mysterious poker chip. Where fear had pegged me to the pew the first time, desperation propelled me to my feet.

I don't remember whom I hugged or what I was wearing or who saw me cry, but I remember how I felt. I was weightless. It was like I'd been wearing heavy chains for so long that they had become a part of me. I hadn't noticed them before, but I could feel when they started coming loose.

I floated back to my seat turning the chip over and over with my fingers. I all but melted into a puddle of tears. Tying myself back down to my seat, I looked at the chip in my hand. Engraved in white on cheap blue plastic were the words:

My grace is sufficient.

Nothing magical happened that night—not in the way I've read about magic: fairy godmothers and sorcerer's wands. Miraculous, yes. Magical, not really. I wasn't put under a spell that would expire at midnight. Instead, my eyes were opened. I was finally able to see and acknowledge the chains on my soul. That's a miracle.

You see, I was still living like those who sat "in darkness and in the shadow of death," a prisoner "in affliction and in irons" but I didn't know it. The Lord let me feel the chains before He let me see them. I was bought by Christ—no longer a slave to sin but to righteousness (Rom. 6:18). But something was still trying to stake its territory in the hidden corners of my mind and heart. Something still "owned" me.

Does something "own" you like it did me? Let me take you through a quick diagnostic:

Have you been hurt in a way that still affects how you live today?

Are you "hooked" on someone or something?

Does the thought of losing whatever or whomever it is give you an anxiety attack?

Are you hung up as I was in sin you just can't shake no matter how hard you try?

If you answered "yes" to any of these questions, there's a good chance you are being temporarily "owned" by something other than Christ. If you're a child of God, He alone is your rightful Lord. But you've found yourself hurt, hooked, or hung up. You've got chains whether you can see them or not; although, I'm pretty sure you can feel them.

HURT

None of us escape life unscathed. We've all at least sustained a few soul wounds. The spectrum of hurt is wide. Perhaps the wounding came from a bully in grade school, a teasing remark in junior high, a move to a new town where you had to start all over, a friendship that fizzled, or just plain old rejection in any form.

On the more severe end, it may have been abuse at the hand of someone who was supposed to care for and love you. Their offense against you is real. They beat you with their words or their fists or both. They violated you in the most vulnerable places and ages. May I pause here and say, I am so sorry. I am not naturally given to tears, but thinking of you and the evil you endured, breaks my heart to the point of real tears.

Here's what I know, even in those dark, hard places, God can redeem. He is not cold-hearted and distant. He is tender-hearted and so very near. When David composed Psalm 56, he was being pursued by Saul whose heart was set on killing him. King Saul was somewhat of a father figure to David. He should have been showing David what it takes to be king since it had been revealed that David would take his place. Instead, Saul viewed David as a threat. He didn't want to give up his crown to some shepherd boy. So he initiated a man-hunt. The target? David, his own son's best friend. When David could have cursed God and shook his fist at the heavens, he chose to compose a lament to God. He reminded himself of the character of the God he worshiped:

You have kept count of my tossings;
put my tears in your bottle.
Are they not in your book?
Then my enemies will turn back
in the day when I call.
This I know, that God is for me. (Ps. 56:8–9)

For those who trust in the Lord, He keeps every tear in His bottle. Not one is forgotten, friend. Not one is diminished in its significance.

No matter where the hurt is on that spectrum, some of us have been cut so deeply that we still feel its ache. Or, maybe the healing process was distorted or incomplete. Either way, we have been indelibly marked by pain—whether relational or physical or both.

We tend to respond in at least two ways to the pain in such a manner that shows we're owned by the wound. First, we can dwell on the offense. The tape runs through our head and we rarely press pause. We let it run, heaping fuel on the fire. We can't get over it because it's as if it just happened—over and over again. Bitterness grows uninhibited in the soil of unforgiveness. There's no way we can let the hurt go seemingly unpunished. Ironically, we're the only ones feeling the beating. As far as we know, the offender is oblivious to the tape rolling in our heads. He or she is utterly unaffected.

The other way we may respond to the hurt is by avoiding it altogether. Tape? What tape? Nothing happened! We're fine! Never mind the lengths at which we go to protect ourselves. We ensure nothing like that can ever happen again.

Needing others becomes something we vow to never fall prey to again. Our remedy to needing people is to be needed instead.

We serve others so that we owe no one but rather they owe us. This makes us feel in control. Everyone is kept at arm's length. To let them in is too dangerous. We pretend to be known while we diligently keep the wound out of sight.

Limping along, we insist everything is fine. The chains drag behind us and we simply cannot figure out what that sound is. We've become so accustomed to the change in our gait, the whitish hue of our scars, that we don't know what it's like to not play the tape nor deny its existence. The hurt owns us.

HOOKED

This is possibly the most obvious state of being "owned." We are hooked on a substance or relationship. When we wake in the morning, it's our first thought. Life without this one thing seems unreasonable at best and impossible at worst. We are convinced that it is absolutely necessary for survival. Everything is a means to this end: getting and keeping the object of our desire. Panic sets in when we feel it's being threatened.

Now, there is a healthy amount of fear in losing someone whom we love dearly. To not fear loss at some level would only reveal that we really never loved them in the first place. Even though I am convinced that the Lord would still be good, loving, and my Provider, my heart quakes at the thought of losing Matt or the kids. The difference is that although I would prefer the Lord keep them safe and alive as long as I am, I know it's not essential to my existence. I don't *need* my husband and kids in order to experience fulfillment on earth. Whom I desperately need is the Lord. Would I mourn? Would I have to be picked up off the ground for weeks, even months? Most definitely! But I would keep going. I would keep breathing in and out God's grace. Remember, His grace is sufficient. It's enough.

The sort of relationship that hooks us isn't like that. It may masquerade as love but it is an obsession. How can we know? First Corinthians 13 tells us what love is like:

Love is patient and kind; love does not envy or boast; it is not arrogant or rude. It does not insist on its own way; it is not irritable or resentful; it does not rejoice at wrongdoing, but rejoices with the truth. Love bears all things, believes all things, hopes all things, endures all things. (1 Cor. 13:4–7)

Let me be honest, I cannot say that I am always patient and kind and that I never struggle with envy or boasting or irritability or resentment. However, true love as described and designed by God is never self-centered, neither is it other-centered. It is God-centered. All the things God calls admirable are listed here: patience, kindness, gratitude, humility, gentleness, truth, and endurance. God is love (1 John 4:8).

I would wager that the relationship that came to mind when I introduced the "hooked" concept to you is not one centered on God. Sure, you may go to church together, call yourselves Christians, and even talk about God, but by all other appearances this relationship is more about fulfilling your desires than it is about reflecting God's glory. More often than not, it is marked by impatience, spite, jealousy, paranoia, harshness, lies, and an on-again, off-again, roller-coaster existence.

If I am describing your marriage, put this book down and call a biblical counselor. Tell your pastor. Get help. By no means am I advising you to divorce your spouse. What I would challenge is your view of the relationship. One of the most perspective-chang-ing and true statements I've ever heard to describe marriage is the subtitle of a book on the subject: "What if God designed marriage to make us holy more than to make us happy?"[1] Marriage is hard but it's not hopeless. It's fulfilling but it's not about us. In fact, it's the most fulfilling when it's not about us but about being a clear picture of God's love for His people—a vision of His steadfast love.

I touched on this briefly at the beginning of this section, but I don't want to gloss over it. Most people who will hold this book in their hands will know Christ. (I know that may not be the case for everyone. If that doesn't describe you, keep reading, my friend! I hope you will find many words of hope to come in the follow-ing pages.) It's fair to assume they are church-belonging, Bible-believing followers of Jesus. What I won't assume is that none of them are hooked on a substance. Addiction is real even within the walls of the church. Alcohol, prescription drugs, recreational drugs, food, cutting, and pornography (visual and emotional, Playboy and explicit romance novels) are not beyond our grasp. They are accessible even to those who call themselves Christians and for some are still a strong temptation. Satan will do what he can to shame us in the dark. The fear of being found out will keep us in our duplicitous life. And we are miserable. We want to stop but we can't. We make rules for ourselves that we consistently bend and break. We decide that we can stop at any time, claiming we just don't really want to right now. We declare our activities acceptable because they're "not really hurting anyone." And all the while, those we love most are alienated by us. They either know our secret or they don't and thus we can't be fully known and loved.

The addiction is a control. When we feel stressed, overwhelmed, sad, lonely, happy, tired, anxious, or scared, we use or indulge to bring our life back under our power. We can't control other things, but we can alter our minds or bodies or escape reality for a few hours. We're hooked.

HUNG UP

For roughly eight years, you could read through my journals and recognize a theme. I would lament my struggle with sin. Then, I would cry out to the Lord, "Help me!" Turn the next page and you'd find the same song, just a different verse: surprise and frustration at my sin, sorrow over it, and crying to the Lord for help. I was a broken record. Even I got tired of singing it.

Running is a cathartic activity for me. The fresh air, the beauty of nature, the sights and sounds of life bustling about me. The steady breathing, my feet keeping time pounding pavement, my muscles contracting and releasing to propel me forward. The privilege of being strong enough to run is not lost on me. I am grateful for the ability. But if you put me inside a gym on a tread-mill, I shrivel. Breathing mysteriously becomes more laborious. My lungs burn obnoxiously sooner. I am convinced someone put lead in my socks. Why is it like this for me? My only guess is that running is meant to get us from point A to point B. Half of running is in our mind. We train our minds by pushing our bodies, proving that we can go farther and harder than our brains believe we can. When I run on the treadmill, my only goal is to finish a certain distance or time. I never leave from a location and I never arrive at a destination so my mind convinces me that I must have gone far enough.

My hang-up with sin is a treadmill jog. I run hard, sweating and barely catching my breath. I look up and I'm exactly where I started. It gets old. I grow weary. Every time I hop on the treadmill my legs are heavier, my time worse. The shackles trip me up and weigh me down. I get nowhere.

THE PROBLEM WITH CHAINS

The problem with chains is that we get used to them. They become so entangled with our identity that we resign to the idea that being hurt, hooked, or hung up is a part of who we are. An encounter with a woman named Donna put flesh on this problem for me.

Donna's appearance hinted at the life she'd lived: her weathered skin, stained and soiled clothes, and hair that hadn't seen a brush in days. Her approach toward us as we exited the pizza parlor was anxious and desperate. Much to my shame, I spoke to my heart, "Not now, I don't have time for this."

"Ma'am? I am so hungry. Could you buy me just a slice of pizza? That's all I want. The man at the grocery store said I couldn't come back there no more. I don't mean to trouble you. I just need somethin' to eat. I'm on parole and they said I can't leave here until I see my officer. And she can't see me until next week. I'm just so hungry. Please?"

We had just paid out at Pizza King and were on a tight schedule to get to Jackson, Mississippi, before midnight. The line to order was out the door and it took an hour for the pizza to bake. They didn't sell it by the slice either. I was at a loss.

My dad walked up as I listened to Donna's story and struggled to decide how to help her. She began stepping backward, waving her hands in front of her, taking a defensive posture as he neared us.

"Sir, I don't want no trouble. Please don't call the cops. I just wanted some pizza. Please, sir. Please!"

Dad's hands came up in reassurance. He meant her no harm. She wasn't easily convinced. She brought out her identification card and flashed it in my face. It indicated that she had recently been released from prison. Her desire was not to harm us but to put all her cards on the table.

It was as if she was saying, I am a felon. I served time in prison. This is who I am.

Matt pulled up in the van ready to load up and head out. Audrey, my oldest, had witnessed the whole encounter. A thought dawned on her and she rushed to the car. As I offered all I could to Donna, directions to a reputable shelter nearby, Audrey handed her a baby bottle full of coins.

The loose change had previously occupied a plastic jar with "New Saddle Fund" scribbled on the front in a 5th grader's handwriting. A pregnancy center in town held a drive to raise funds for their cause. They passed out empty baby bottles to fill with cash, coins, or a check, whatever one could do to help. We kept forgetting to drop it at the front desk at church so it was still sitting in our van.

"Take this," Audrey said.

"I can't take this baby's bottle!"

I assured her that this is how grace comes. It humbles. There's nothing we can do but receive it with gratitude. A dam broke. Tears, cries, and heavy sighs rushed out of Donna. She fell back against the wall and slid down to her seat. Her head down between her knees, Audrey and I laid our hands on her and offered up a prayer to the God who knows Donna, the God who sees her.

There was so much more I wanted to do for Donna but it was what I could do, what I was to do, for that time and place. I think of her often and entrust her to the Lord.

What I can't shake from my few minutes with Donna is the snapshot of her waving the ID in front of me. Before her time in prison maybe she was known as a wife, a mother, a daughter, a sister, a coworker, or a neighbor. Now, she's a felon. She didn't just accept it, she absorbed it.

Our chains are connected to who we are, but they don't have to stay that way. The Lord of steadfast love is able to break any chain—if we are willing. He invites us to trace them back to the source and watch Him work.

CHAPTER SEVEN

Broken

The Israelites' history reads like a more serious and tragic version of the movie *Groundhog Day*. In case you've forgotten this gem (or you were born after 1990), Bill Murray stars as Phil Conners, a weatherman from Pittsburgh who is assigned to report on the iconic emergence of the Punxsutawney, Pennsylvania, groundhog for the fourth year in a row. He arrives with little enthusiasm and a lot of frustration, which he makes abundantly clear. The story is entirely beneath him. This year, though, is set apart. A blizzard hits the town and leaves Phil stranded in misery for an extra night—or so he thinks. He awakes the next morning to find it's Groundhog Day. Again. He mistakes it for the most massive case of déjà vu ever. However, the following day he experiences it again, and again, and again with no escape. Since Phil is stuck in the perpetual cycle, he attempts to make the most of his situation—nobly at times and not so much at others.

When reading through Scripture, we see a "Groundhog Day" phenomenon. The Israelites call upon the name of the Lord, and He responds in steadfast love. The people stray and worship other gods. The Lord sends a prophet to warn the people. He calls out their sin and calls them to repentance. The people ignore and sometimes scoff at the prophet's words. In His mercy (yes, His mercy), He allows the Israelites to be conquered by another nation. They despair of life and call out to the Lord for rescue. The Lord fulfills His promise to be faithful to them. They repent and return to the Lord. Life moves on and the people forget, again. They turn away. They rebel. The Lord warns. The people disbelieve. They are conquered. They cry for help. The Lord delivers. They return. And then they forget. Again. It's a broken record that plays the first verse over and over again. How patient is the Lord!

SUPPRESSING THE TRUTH

"Some sat in darkness and in the shadow of death, prisoners in affliction and in irons, for they had rebelled against the words of God, and spurned the counsel of the Most High" (Ps. 107:10–11).

How did the people in Psalm 107 end up in chains? It says they had rebelled against the words of God and spurned the counsel of the Most High. They knew what was right and good but resisted doing so. The apostle Paul fleshes this out for us in Romans 1:18–23:

> For the wrath of God is revealed from heaven against all ungodliness and unrighteousness of men, who by their unrighteousness suppress the truth. For what can be known about God is plain to them, because God has shown it to them. For his invisible attributes, namely, his eternal power and divine nature, have been clearly perceived, ever since the creation of the world, in the things that have been made. So they are without excuse. For although they knew God, they did not honor him as God or give thanks to him, but they became futile in their thinking, and their foolish hearts were darkened. Claiming to be wise, they became fools, and exchanged the glory of the immortal God for images resembling mortal man and birds and animals and creeping things.

Whether we want to admit it or not, when we look up at the sky or out over the ocean or toward the mountains, there is something nagging us deep inside. Something that says, there's more. There's Someone behind all of this. This isn't an accident. Not only is there the nagging, the Lord equipped us with a conscience even when, from the day we're born until the day we meet Christ, we are marked by Adam's sin. In our fallenness, we still have a sense of right and wrong. I remember the first time I was acutely aware of wrong, specifically my wrong.

A sweet little lady and her husband lived directly behind my favorite house growing up. If you didn't know better, you would have thought they'd plopped their home right in the back corner of our lot. We were that close.

One afternoon, my brother, Jonathan, and I had a rare moment of peaceful play—we were usually at odds with each other. Our neighbor called to us from her backyard. We bounded to the fence line hoping for a treat, or an invitation to see the inside of her house (which only our imaginations had visited). Her wrinkles bunched into a smile, "Now aren't y'all the sweetest? So loving to each other!"

I knew better. I was anything but kind to my little brother. We fought like cats and dogs. The only time we didn't was when we were apart. As I look back, I lament the discord. Even then, my eight-year-old heart knew the truth. Sure, my parents instructed us to get along, but I didn't really need them to tell me that. I knew it was wrong. I knew I treated him badly no matter how justified I felt in the moment. Somewhere along the way I had "suppressed the truth." One comment from that precious woman sent the truth rising to the top, and I couldn't push it down anymore.

In Psalm 107, it appears that not only did they have this innate sense of a Creator and of right and wrong described in Romans, but they knew the words and counsel of God. This is an explicit knowledge, not just implicit. They had heard from the mouths of the prophets, God's chosen messengers, and still failed to acknowledge God. They claimed to be wise but became fools. They were convinced that they knew better than God—that they had it all under control.

Essentially, that's what being hurt, hooked, or hung up is about: a desire to be in control. We make vows:

> I will never be hurt again.
> I will never know happiness without this one thing.
> I will get it right.

Futile—that's what Paul writes under the inspiration of the Holy Spirit. It's futile to vow to not be hurt again. Who can control that? It's futile to think a substance, relationship, or habit can sustain our happiness. It will fail. And it's futile to white-knuckle our way through life. For whom has that worked? Who, apart from Christ, has gotten it right?

MOST HIGH

I don't believe it's a coincidence that in the psalm God is referred to here as "the Most High." In chapter 1, I pointed out that for the most part God is referred to as the LORD, Yahweh, the most personal, intimate name for God throughout the psalm. "Most High" is no less true, but it's interesting to note it's occurrence here. In Hebrew, the word is *elyown*. You'll be surprised that the definition for this Hebrew word is "most high." Mind-blowing.

When someone or something is the most high, it means there's nothing higher. (I did a lot of research on this—you're welcome.) If we think about being "most high," there are two ideas inherently connected: perspective and power. To be most high is to have the best perspective and the most power.

The relationship between position and perspective is spelled out in Isaiah 55:9: "For as the heavens are higher than the earth, so are my ways higher than your ways and my thoughts than your thoughts." Picture yourself on the 20th floor of a high-rise. You look down on a vehicle below. There's a family sitting in their van in heavy traffic. You watch the driver take a turn down an alley to avoid the congestion; but from your perspective, you can see that their decision is in vain. The route they chose to circumvent the problem will actually send them to a dead end. Your "higher" perspective gives you an advantage over the family on the ground stuck in traffic. If the family had had your perspective, they would have known that their "short-cut" was in reality the shortest distance to a dead-end.

You lament that you had no power to tell them. You didn't know who they were so you couldn't call them on your cell. You also had no way to intervene physically. You couldn't turn the vehicle for them. With God Most High, however, He is never lacking power.

Psalm 115:3 illustrates the connection between position and power: "Our God is in the heavens; he does all that he pleases." In the psalmist's mind there's nothing higher than the heavens. It would be like us saying, "God is outside space and time; He does all that He pleases." He is the Creator of all things. You'll recall in chapter 1 that He is "I AM WHO I AM." He is the all-powerful One—sovereign over all. He doesn't sit on the 20th floor with us down below wishing He could do something. He has the power to intervene—to change our route or change the traffic. The beautiful part is that He always knows what action would be best. He is the Lord fueled by steadfast love. He knows what's best (perspective) and is able to do what's best (power). He is God Most High.

When we see "Most High" in the New Testament, the words are usually coming from the mouths of other-worldly beings: angels and demons. An angel appears to Mary in Luke 1:32 claiming that she will bear a son who will be great and "will be called Son of the Most High." He goes on to say that the Holy Spirit will come upon her and "the power of the Most High will overshadow you" (Luke 1:35).

The angel knows God is Most High because he is a messenger of God. He, as an inferior, has received his assignments from God and knows he is expected to obey. Just as a private receives and follows through with orders from a higher-ranking officer, so also the angel perceives and responds to God. There's no one superior to God who can change the angel's orders.

The Gospels also record demons addressing God as Most High. In Mark 5:7, a demon-possessed man cries out, "What have you to do with me, Jesus, Son of the Most High God?" In Acts 16:17, a girl possessed by an evil spirit follows Paul and other disciples, crying out "these men are servants of the Most High God, who proclaim to you the way of salvation."

What's unnerving about this is that even the demons refer to Him accurately and yet this doesn't change their relationship to Him. We can call Him "Most High God." We can believe He is all-knowing and all-powerful but until we acknowledge that He is good and trustworthy and relinquish our control, we will keep lugging our chains behind us.

BOWED HEARTS AND HARD LABOR

"So he bowed their hearts down with hard labor; they fell down, with none to help" (Ps. 107:12).

He bowed their hearts down? This doesn't sound like a good and trustworthy God—at least from our limited perspective. When we are hurt, hooked, or hung up and trying our hardest to exert control, we are essentially believing that we are higher than God. Our hearts are exalting ourselves above Him. They are proud and in the wrong place, needing to be humbled because we are not the Most High. We don't have the best perspective nor the power to really do anything about anything. It is loving and merciful of God to put us in our place because we wreck it all.

Remember the Israelites in Egypt? How they forgot that Egypt wasn't the point? That there was a land God promised to show them? Remember how Pharaoh forgot about Joseph? "Therefore they set taskmasters over them to afflict them with heavy burdens" (Exod. 1:11). Remember how this led the people to groan?

The people of Israel groaned because of their slavery and cried out for help. Their cry for rescue from slavery came up to God. And God heard their groaning, and God remembered his covenant with Abraham, with Isaac, and with Jacob. God saw the people of Israel—and God knew. (Exod. 2:23–25)

Remember how He sent Moses to Pharaoh saying, "Let my people go!"? And how things got worse before they got better?

The same day Pharaoh commanded the taskmasters of the people and their foremen, "You shall no longer give the people straw to make bricks, as in the past; let them go and gather straw for

> themselves. But the number of bricks that they made in the past
> you shall impose on them, you shall by no means reduce it, for
> they are idle. Therefore they cry, 'Let us go and offer sacrifice
> to our God.' Let heavier work be laid on the men that they may
> labor at it and pay no regard to lying words." (Exod. 5:6–9)

They had cried out because of their slavery and God heard and knew. Since He is God Most High, wouldn't He have known how Pharaoh would respond? Yes, and He did. Because God does not waste opportunities, we can trust He was working to accomplish something. Maybe it's because the Israelites groaned more over their chains than their rebellious hearts. So He sent "hard labor" to bow them even lower. To turn their gaze toward the chains on their hearts, not just the chains on their wrists and ankles.

In His steadfast love, He will do the same with us. He will lovingly make that hurt sting. He will press His eternally powerful finger on that wound to show He's not done there. He will let you hit rock bottom with that substance or relationship. He will let you grow tired and weary of trying to get it right in your own strength. The "hard labor" will force us to look at the chains around our hearts, if we'd be willing to see.

SLAVE TO SON

"Then they cried to the LORD in their trouble, and he delivered them from their distress" (Ps. 107:13).

Only God Most High is able to break our chains. All our working and striving or looking to others for help fails. The weeds of rebellion have sunk their roots deep. We need Someone strong enough to pull them out completely. The Someone inserted another One into the story who would take us from slave to son:

But when the fullness of time had come, God sent
forth his Son, born of woman, born under the law,
to redeem those who were under the law, so that we
might receive adoption as sons. (Gal. 4:4–5)

The Law—what Moses brought down from the mountain on tablets of stone—showed us just how much we couldn't keep it. We were slaves to it without even knowing it. The Law shows us what is and reveals to us that we are utterly unable to keep it.

"You shall have no other gods before me" (Deut. 5:7). There are no other gods but the Lord.

"You shall not make for yourself a carved image, or any likeness of anything that is in heaven above, or that is on the earth beneath, or that is in the water under the earth. You shall not bow down to them or serve them" (Deut. 5:8–9).

Even the gods we fashion with our own hands will not be enough.

"You shall not take the name of the LORD your God in vain" (Deut. 5:11).

His name is the most valuable, most precious, most powerful. It carries so much weight that it is impossible to throw it around irreverently even when it seems we might.

"Observe the Sabbath day, to keep it holy, as the LORD your God commanded you" (Deut. 5:12).

We need rest. God made us so.

"Honor your father and your mother" (Deut. 5:16).

The Lord gives us parents for our good (even though they may shirk their responsibility) because we aren't born knowing all we will. We need guidance so "that [our] days may be long, and that it may go well with" us (Deut. 5:16).

"You shall not murder" (Deut. 5:17).

"And you shall not commit adultery" (Deut. 5:18).

"And you shall not steal" (Deut. 5:19).

"And you shall not bear false witness against your neighbor (Deut. 5:20).

"And you shall not covet your neighbor's wife" (Deut. 5:21).

These last five are obvious. Murder, adultery, robbery, lying, and coveting wreak all sorts of havoc.

Our chains show us that we have broken the very first commandment. We are "owned." Something besides God has become our god. The slavery goes further than skin-deep. It pierces all the way through to our hearts. Just as we did in the desert, we do so in chains. We cry out to God for deliverance. Not to be delivered from pain but from our chains. A true cry for help rises from our lips when we can acknowledge our rebellion and inability to free ourselves.

So Christ came, born under the Law like us. Human. But He kept it perfectly where we failed entirely. He redeemed us, Scripture says. He bought us as slaves with His own blood so that we could be adopted as sons and daughters.

For those who have been bought, who are already sons and daughters, why do we still act like slaves?

"For freedom Christ has set us free; stand firm therefore, and do not submit again to a yoke of slavery" (Gal. 5:1).

"He brought them out of darkness and the shadow of death, and burst their bonds apart." (Ps. 107:14)

OUT OF DARKNESS

The dark can hide all kinds of ugly. The light fixture in our master bathroom did a good job of lighting the room but left much to be desired aesthetically. No fear, online shopping is near! I clicked on a lovely substitute, dropped it in the digital basket, and checked out. My purchase would arrive only a few days later.

The box was a bit smaller than what I expected, but I gave a shrug and bounced to the bathroom. I set it aside until our friend Ron could install it. He arrived with tools in hand. I didn't want to be in his way so I busied myself in the kitchen. Once the installation was complete, Ron called to me. I couldn't wait to see the beauty hanging above our mirror.

My wide-eyed smile folded into a furrowed brow.

"This can't be right."

The light fixture might as well have been a night-light. I could barely see a thing! Was that a freckle or a blemish? Was my hair dirty blonde or black? I couldn't tell.

I haven't had the heart to tell Matt that I chose poorly nor to inform Ron that his work was somewhat in vain. So any time I really want to see to put my makeup on, I go to my daughters' bathroom. They have a large window and bright lights that show me everything my mirror doesn't. I'll be honest, at times I'm afraid to go in their bathroom. I fear what I may find on my face that has been obvious to everyone else: a weird hair or blemish or something worse.

To be brought into the light can be frightening. It means we will have to face what we haven't had the courage to acknowledge. We will see the ugly with our own eyes. We will see our rebellion. We will see every jagged edge of that hurt, every hideous consequence of our obsession, and every grotesque inadequacy.

Just because something is scary doesn't mean it's bad. First John 1:5–8 says,

God is light, and in him is no darkness at all. If we say we have fellowship with him while we walk in darkness, we lie and do not practice the truth. But if we walk in the light, as he is in the light, we have fellowship with one another, and the blood of Jesus his Son cleanses us from all sin. If we say we have no sin, we deceive ourselves, and the truth is not in us.

God is illuminating light. If He is light, then we know light is good. What does it mean to walk in the light? It means we stand in front of the well-lit bathroom and look. We invite others to look with us. We tell the hurt. We expose what's hooked us. We confess all the ways we can't get it right.

After I had the courage to take the blue poker chip, I entered a step program. We had chants. We introduced ourselves, "Hi, my name is _____ and I struggle with _____." We worked out of little booklets that asked the most intrusive questions. It was amazing.

For this people-pleasing perfectionist, I needed something quirky that stepped all over my polished toes. Nine other women and I circled our chairs in a back room of the church and stammered the answers to our questions. I recall one session when I was afraid to carry my response on sound waves, to give voice to a deep, dark secret. I feared the atmosphere wouldn't be able to handle it and would rip in two. To my surprise, the air held together when I brought the secret to light. Even more astonishing, the women with whom I shared didn't look at me like I had grown an extra head. They nodded compassionately and we went on to the next person.

I was shocked and simultaneously relieved. My ugly was out in the open and no one recoiled. They knew they had their own ugly, and they knew Christ's blood is enough to cover us both.

I walked in the light where God already is. I had fellowship with Him and others. I found His grace was enough to cover, cleanse, ransom, and redeem.

OUT OF THE SHADOW OF DEATH

The Lord not only brings us out of darkness, He brings us out of the shadow of death. Each of my kids has gone through a stage where they are mesmerized by their shadow. Usually, it's when they're at a toddling age. A summer sunset lures us to the driveway. We press bare feet on warm concrete, dancing to the hum of locusts. A faint figure synchronizes its steps with the child. He anxiously giggles picking one foot high off the ground and waving an arm above his head. It's like him but it's not him—a shadow.

Chains are like death but not yet death. Make no mistake, unless the Lord delivers us from the chains of the rebellion of unbelief, we will die (spiritually and physically). But when He delivers us from the chains, we will feel like we've been brought back to life.

This sounds exciting and hopeful, and it is. However, the reality is that dead things can't feel. And feeling is entirely different from not feeling. (You know the feeling.) Like when your foot is wedged under your other leg sitting crisscross on the ground and you stand up to let the nerves reorient themselves, and it's all pins and needles, and you regret standing up? But if you hadn't, who knows if your foot would have fallen off right there on your living room floor and you wouldn't have known because you forgot it was even attached? Feeling after not feeling is like that. It hurts at first.

You aren't numbing the pain by setting up an impenetrable wall around your heart. You aren't tempering all feeling with a substance or relationship. You're finally willing to be undone without making it all right.

The feelings start taking over. You discover the height of joy but also the depth of disappointment. Your cold stone heart is replaced with warm flesh, susceptible to scarring. It's terrifying. But there's good news:

"And I will give you a new heart, and a new spirit I will put within you. And I will remove the heart of stone from your flesh and give you a heart of flesh. And I will put my Spirit within you, and cause you to walk in my statutes and be careful to obey my rules. You shall dwell in the land that I gave to your fathers, and you shall be my people, and I will be your God." (Ezek. 36:26–28)

The new heart of flesh will beat wildly for Him. His Spirit will cause us to walk, not in rebellious chains, but in glorious obedience. He will be our God. Any trauma our new heart will take will only be what He allows for our good and His glory.

BURSTING

Not one house I grew up in was left untouched by my parents. They were the Chip and Joanna of their time.[1] Mom had all the vision and a little bit of elbow grease to lend while Dad did most of the heavy lifting. Mom made the plan; Dad executed it. There were always dreams of what could be added or changed. The possibilities were endless. The renovation gene passed down to me but, bless his heart, Matt couldn't care less. He has more of the "if it isn't broken, don't fix it" mentality.

So when I poured out all the plans bubbling inside my homemaking heart to him, he did what any other man would do. He called my dad. The first project they joined forces in completing was a covered deck on the back of our house. It was beautiful. I was so proud of Matt. You'll be glad to know that it's still standing.

As invigorating as the deck building was for Matt, he'd much rather drop by on demolition day. Rolling up his sleeves, gripping the handle of a sledgehammer, and swinging away brings him more joy than meticulously sanding a piece of wood. I can't help but think that the Lord possesses that kind of joy in bursting our bonds apart. And bursting? Isn't that something that happens with explosives? I imagine God speaking the bursting apart. If He can form creation by the word of His mouth, I believe He can undo it just the same.

God delights in setting you free, friend. The broken record of bondage doesn't have to keep playing. You can break free. Cry out to the God Most High, the One who brings darkness to light and dead to life. The only One who can set you free.

PART FOUR

Folly

(PSALM 107:17–22)

Some were fools through their sinful ways,
and because of their iniquities suffered affliction;
they loathed any kind of food,
and they drew near to the gates of death.
Then they cried to the LORD in their trouble,
and he delivered them from their distress.
He sent out his word and healed them,
and delivered them from their destruction.
Let them thank the LORD for his steadfast love,
for his wondrous works to the children of man!
And let them offer sacrifices of thanksgiving,
and tell of his deeds in songs of joy!

CHAPTER EIGHT

Foolish

"If this is your first time to drive a moped or you have limited experience, please do not rent it."

Well, I'm out.

If the owner of the moped rental company was pleading with us not to hand money over to ride one of his vehicles, he must mean business. What shocked me more than the owner's plea was Matt's nod and resolute posture. Arms folded, eyes forward, head bobbing up and down, he seemed confident that his moped experience was sufficient.

I was shocked because, at that point, we had been married for over fifteen years and together for seventeen, and I could hardly recall a time I'd seen him straddling one much less driving it. He answered my sideways glance.

"I used to drive Blake Chilton's back in college."

My worries were not immediately quelled. Out of respect for him and because we were with a group of friends, I conceded and trusted that he knew what he was doing. The owner pulled three mopeds out from a large metal container.

When he rolled out the maroon one with scratches all over the front and sides, I prayed, "Dear Lord, please don't let that be ours."

"Chandler!" he called, tapping the seat of the maroon moped, "This one's yours."

I whispered a prayer to the Lord, "Preserve our lives!"

Or something like that.

Matt swung one leg over, settled in, and reacquainted himself with the controls. My eagerness, however, did not match Matt's. I sat down and carefully placed my feet on the pegs. I slipped my arms around Matt and squeezed.

"Baby, I can't breathe."

"Oops. Sorry!"

Our friends led the way. The plan was to take in the island views via scooter, stop off at a few points of interest, and arrive at our final destination to dine for lunch alfresco. The mopeds were equipped with the most powerful engines appropriate for a scooter. We could feel its capability as Matt gassed it up an incline. What we didn't realize was that the road curved sharply just beyond the highest point. Instead of hugging the turn, we continued our path straight into the lane of oncoming traffic and to the edge of the road (where it dropped off significantly). Matt squeezed the brake and instinctively pressed his feet on the asphalt to provide drag and help us stop. I was no help at all. I'm not sure I was even able to catch my breath to say a word. With my heart beating through my chest, I was finally able to breathe out, "Are you okay?"

We were visibly shaken. At the same time, we were incredibly grateful. The Lord had protected us as there was no traffic coming our way to plow into us. He had spared our lives.

Matt and I knew what we should have done at that moment. We should have turned around and cautiously made our way back to the rental office. But we didn't.

As we returned to the correct side of the road, I argued with myself.

Should I ask Matt if he really is qualified to drive this thing?

You're just going to sound like a nag, Lauren.

But what if we really get hurt?

You don't trust Matt?

I resigned to go with the flow.

Surely that will be the only hiccup.

Matt will figure out how much gas to give, and we'll both feel which way to lean into a curve.

Once we caught up with our friends, they pulled to the side to make sure we were okay and to consult the map for our next move. The rules of the road on this particular island were influenced by the British meaning they drive on the left side. This complicated our route. There was a right turn we needed to make to continue on our way, but it was a heavily traveled intersection in which one lane of traffic did not stop.

My anxiety intensified as we noticed red and blue flashing lights at the intersection. Two cars were pulled to the side. It appeared there had been a fender-bender. The officer stood beside the cars, examining the damage and taking notes. Their presence further narrowed the lane we were attempting to join (and further fueled my apprehension).

Our friends edged out, successfully making the turn. I let out a sigh of relief. If they could make it, I thought, we could too. Matt saw an opening and took it. He knew the turn would be more shallow than he'd like because of the cars pulled to the side, but he was confident.

What he didn't count on was the gravel heaped in the middle of the road. Our back tire hit the patch and slid out from under us. I felt gravity pull us onto our right side. My head hit the asphalt with such force that the world vibrated. A goose egg grew immediately just under the edge of the skull cap I was wearing. I don't remember how, but aside from my head hitting the ground, I never laid completely down on the road. My feet seemed to find their way underneath me instantly. My first thought was to let Matt know that I was okay.

He made his way over to me, his knees bleeding and palms gashed. We were so relieved to be alive. Our friends had turned around to assess our condition, comfort, and help us. They called the moped company so they could dispatch assistance. My head throbbed and stomach turned.

Matt inspected the damage to the scooter and our persons. I could feel my tank top sticking to places all over my back. I dreaded to peel it away and look.

Help finally arrived. The moped was loaded up in a truck to be repaired, and we were driven back to the ship.

Did I mention this was our first full day on a cruise?

All my dreams of soaking up the sun on deck and splashing in the ocean when at port were dashed as the ship physician examined us.

"First, you need to go back to your stateroom and run the shower over the wounds. Once I bandage you up, you'll need to keep it clean and dry. No sweat. No water. No sun."

We trudged down the hall to our room, wincing with each step. Road rash covered a good portion of both of our backs. We cringed at the thought of running anything over our wounds, much less water. If we were to get it clean and remove the gravel, we had little choice.

I won't lie to you. Few things have hurt as badly as willingly streaming water over raw skin. It might as well have been lava.

There was little romance for the rest of our vacation aside from applying antibiotic cream all over each other's oozing burns. We walked around like mummies—wrapped in gauze, awkwardly shifting weight from one foot to the other as we walked, arms unnaturally far from our sides. We laid down each night giggling (and simultaneously wincing) at the sight of us. We may have been in excruciating pain, but we were grateful to be alive.

The Lord was gracious to spare our lives despite our folly. In his commentary on the Psalms, Spurgeon points out that, "Many sicknesses are the direct result of foolish acts."[1] Our sickness, our pain, was a direct result of our foolish act. After the first brush with death, we should have admitted the moped was too much for us. I should have swallowed the fear of being a nag and nudged Matt to consider returning the scooter. Matt should have recognized that his previous experience was not enough to handle this type of moped.[2]

But we didn't. Our pride wouldn't let us be the Debbie Downers of the group, and we paid the price. Our foolishness made us suffer.

FOLLY

What exactly is folly? It has such an old-fashioned ring to it, doesn't it? Though it is an ancient notion, it's very much alive and well in our modern times. Folly is essentially earthly wisdom. It says: *God, I know You made me and thus You know what's best, but I know how life should really work.*

Proverbs 9:13 depicts earthly wisdom in this way:

The woman Folly is loud;
she is seductive and knows nothing.

May I make a note before we move on? Although folly is referred to as a woman here, it is by no means limited to females. Likewise, when we dig into what the proverbs have to say about wisdom, it's personified by a woman again. And we can humbly admit that women do not have the market cornered on wisdom.

Let's take our cues on folly from this text (despite the form she may take). First of all, she's loud. You can't not hear her.

Loud

If you've ever met my husband in real life or heard him through a podcast, you'd emphatically agree that he has a "voice that carries." The Lord knew what He was doing when He stitched those vocal folds together. He knew they would need to be powerful enough to preach for long periods of time multiple times a day. For whatever reason, though, the decibels rise exponentially when he's talking on the phone. Compound that with a crowded space (like a busy restaurant or car full of kids) and ears start ringing.

One such occurrence took place in a bustling (and tiny) Chinese restaurant. Matt had been waiting for an important call. His phone rang as we were being escorted to our table. He answered in his usual booming voice and continued the conversation in the same manner. We passed a table where a woman turned to her husband and said (not so subtly), "He's so loud!" Ironically, Matt heard her over the person he was talking to as well as his own voice. We still laugh thinking about it.

I imagine the woman was having a nice, somewhat quiet lunch with her family when a voice hijacked their conversation. She had no choice but to eavesdrop on Matt's phone call. To her, he was that loud.

Folly has "a voice that carries." We don't have to press in or bend down to hear her. Hers is the voice I hear first and loudest. It sounds a lot like mine:

I deserve better.

They should get what they have coming. I should receive mercy.

Are you kidding me? Don't they know they have a blinker? Use it! I'm not a mind-reader!

Seductive

Volume isn't the only characteristic of Folly that grabs our attention. The Proverbs say she's seductive. She entices us with the promise of all (we think) we could want.

I am the point.

Life is about me.

I'll be honest. I want life to be about me. I want to be the point. Nowhere is that more apparent than when I'm behind the wheel. I want every green light but only if I'm in a hurry. If I want to text someone or read an e-mail or browse through Instagram, I want a nice, long red light. It's almost a guarantee that I will get exactly the opposite. In a hurry? Every light is red. Taking my time? Green. I am convinced the universe is against me.

Not only do I want the world to revolve around me, I want the Lord to be my short-order cook, not the holy God that He is. Since I'm the point and life is about me, even God should be at my disposal. He exists to make my plans happen—quickly and to my specifications.

Although I have an infinitely more limited view of my own life than He does, I am convinced that I know how my life should go. The blessings and ease afforded to my neighbor? *I'll take that with a side of a long, painless existence.* The opportunity given to that person? *I'm afraid our orders were mixed up. Fix it now or you can forget further compliance from me.*

"Now" is Folly's refrain. Our hearts and minds are set on now, what feels good now, what we want now without thinking about how our actions will bear on the future. She adopts the motto: eat, drink, and be merry. Translation: this is all there is so live it up. Consequences? What are those?

On a recent trip, I picked up a copy of *Texas Monthly* and thumbed through the articles. One caught my attention. As I read, I realized the story was a clear picture of Folly's infatuation with the here and now as well as its ability to infect its surroundings.

The Highlands is an area just northeast of Houston, Texas. There's nothing especially noteworthy about this suburb. On the surface, it appears to blend right in to the urban sprawl. Underneath, it's bubbling with toxins. Literally.

Two miles south of the town lies the San Jacinto waste pits, an area on the Environmental Protection Agency's National Priorities list because of its high toxicity. Forty years ago, a paper company contracted a waste management company to dispose of their industrial waste. They dumped the toxic waste where they had dug pits along the San Jacinto River. Once the pits were full, the area was abandoned. Slowly, the land between the pits and the river began to erode, allowing the toxins to seep into the river. In 2008, Hurricane Ike hit only miles away from the pits, flooding the area and further distributing poisons throughout the Highlands community. Residents began falling mysteriously ill—lymphoma, multiple myeloma, and lupus, among others. The faulty manner in which the waste was disposed showed little care for the future. This lack of forethought resulted in sickness of every kind. Folly brought forth affliction.

Affliction

Psalm 107 tells us that the people in folly "suffered affliction." The affliction may manifest physically, emotionally, or both. When we're operating in earthly wisdom, anchoring our hearts in what we say is right and good rather than what God has declared to be right and good, the most common response is anxiety.

We are overwhelmed with the weight of the world. We've put ourselves on God's throne, making decrees and falling miserably short. We feel our inadequacy and inability to sustain life. We are not God. We are not the point of life. God is not our short-order cook. This is not all there is. Life reveals these truths pretty quickly. Folly refuses to accept it.

When I refuse to accept truth and continue to operate in folly, then bitterness, jealousy, anger, and selfish ambition abound. The sickness in my heart starts spilling over into my life. My words are seasoned with resentment. I peer through gloomy-colored glasses. I look for opportunities to justify my jealousy and anger. All of my time is spent considering how my life is affected. I can't see beyond myself.

My Folly

There have been several seasons of folly for me. I wish I could paint a different picture for you, but that would be dishonest and, ultimately, a disservice. You see, no one is immune to folly. Not even a pastor's wife.

At the center of my seasons of folly has been a distrust of the Lord and an unwillingness to yield to His leading. During those times, I buy into earthly wisdom entirely. I touched on the beginning of one such season in chapter 2. It all started in the "desert," but I neglected to continue crying out to the Lord. Instead of turning outward and upward to Him, I turned inward and downward toward myself. I manipulated and maneuvered, strove and strained to make life work according to my plan.

I recognized that the Lord had given me the desire to lead people in worship through song and the ability to do so, but I wanted to call the shots on how He would use me. I looked at women around me—women who were doing what I wanted to do. I pointed my finger at them and ordered, "I'll take that, Lord."

I wanted that voice.

I wanted that platform.

I wanted that record deal.

I wanted that admiration.

His plan didn't look like mine though. He had something else in mind for me. My feet were nearly bruised and bloodied from kicking against Him. I even suffered physically. The stress of not resting in His plan manifested in fatigue and irritability. I had no peace. Toxic pride and folly flowed unchecked, and I was unrepentant. They seeped into my life, infecting everything.

I couldn't rejoice with those who were receiving even a hint of what I desired. My words tore down. If they were seeing the fulfillment of what I wanted, I had to do something about it. I had to dismantle their dream coming true since mine wasn't. All my focus was on what I didn't have.

Opportunities to serve and be blessed in the serving were all around, but I didn't have eyes to see them. I only saw what I didn't have—what I couldn't have. I was like a toddler sitting in my highchair, tight-lipped and protesting a bite of pureed green beans; all the while, insisting on a meal of ice cream and cotton candy.

Food

Psalm 107:18 says "they loathed any kind of food." I was loathing real food. What I demanded was fake food—junk food. I didn't want what the Lord so graciously provided.

When the Israelites wandered in the wilderness and God provided manna and quail for them, they were just about as grateful as I was. Numbers 11:4–6 describes their plight:

Now the rabble that was among them had a strong craving. And the people of Israel also wept again and said, "Oh that we had meat to eat! We remember the fish we ate in Egypt that cost nothing, the cucumbers, the melons, the leeks, the onions, and the garlic. But now our strength is dried up, and there is nothing at all but this manna to look at."

A few things to note in this passage of Scripture are indiscernible from the text alone. You may think, *Yeah, God. You've asked too much of these people. They're wandering the desert and all they want are a few fish, some fruit, and vegetables! It's not much, and really, who can last on wafers and little birds? And You're God. This would be easy for You to whip up out of nowhere!*

What God sees clearly here may not be apparent to us at first blush. Who is this "rabble" among the people of Israel? They were those who had intermarried with the Egyptians. This wasn't an ethnicity issue. It was a trust issue.

This group of people symbolized Israel's propensity to trust man rather than God. In taking Egyptians as husbands or wives, they were essentially buying into earthly wisdom. They placed themselves back on the throne to reign and rule their own lives, to be the point and to only consider the here and now. What they couldn't see from the vantage point of their wedding day in Egypt was the refining heat of the wilderness—when their faith would be tested. The trust they had put in Egypt, in man, would rear its head as a rabble, a loud minority stirring up trouble and revealing Israel's folly.

The Israelites had a false perception of reality. God provided exactly what they needed for free. No labor was demanded to reap it. The manna appeared in the morning and the quail came on its own. There was no toil in it for them, nor an exchange of goods. Egypt's bounty? The cucumbers, melons, leeks, onions and garlic? Their price tag? Harsh servitude, enslavement—their very lives.

Remember when Jesus was tempted by Satan in the wilderness? The enemy prodded Him to turn a rock into bread. But Jesus responded: "It is written, 'Man shall not live by bread alone, but by every word that comes from the mouth of God'" (Matt. 4:4). God's Word is the real food. But when we're stuck in a season of folly, we have no appetite for it. Our palates are accustomed to the empty calories of earthly wisdom. We feed on nothing, wasting away bit by bit and bite by bite. We draw near to the gates of death.

Folly resembles what comes most natural. She's easy to hear and our flesh likes what she says. So how do we escape her hypnotic hold? How do we forsake the toxic and empty and embrace the healthy and full?

It starts with fear.

CHAPTER NINE

Wisdom

The fear of the Lord is the beginning of wisdom,
and the knowledge of the Holy One is insight. (Prov. 9:10)

The opposite of folly is wisdom—true wisdom, not earthly. Scripture tells us that the beginning of wisdom is the fear of the Lord. How can this be? Isn't fear something we're supposed to reject? Doesn't Romans 8 say that we are no longer slaves to fear but have received the Spirit of adoption as sons? Why should we fear now that we are free?

A moment between our good friends Moses and the Israelites sheds light on what it means to fear the Lord:

Now when all the people saw the thunder and the flashes of
lightning and the sound of the trumpet and the mountain
smoking, the people were afraid and trembled, and they stood far
off and said to Moses, "You speak to us, and we will listen; but
do not let God speak to us, lest we die." Moses said to the people,
"Do not fear, for God has come to test you, that the fear of him
may be before you, that you may not sin." (Exod. 20:18–20)

The Israelites had just heard the Lord speak the Ten Commandments. Not in a way that we may say we "heard God speak"—something that is more of a prompting of the Holy Spirit rather than an audible voice. With their very own ears, they perceived the voice of God. What a terrifying privilege.

John Piper interprets Moses' exhortation to the people:

The fear that Moses was telling them to get rid of was the fear of coming close to God and hearing his voice. The fear that Moses wanted them to keep before their eyes was that God is fearfully powerful and opposed to sin. The fear of kindling God's powerful wrath against sin ought not to drive us away from God but to God for mercy.[1]

To even begin to have wisdom, we need an intimate understanding of the fear of the Lord. According to the passage in Exodus 20, we are to reject the fear of coming close to God and hearing His voice. In fact, Psalm 107 describes those in folly doing just what those in the desert and in chains did. They cried out to the Lord.

Once again they humbled themselves. They recognized that their earthly wisdom wasn't working. And they drew near. Their wisdom had dried up—they knew that they didn't know. But they knew they could know the One who does. No longer looking inward and downward, they looked outward and upward to Him.

"SEEING" GOD

To rightly fear God, we must rightly see Him. This goes back to calling on Him as "the LORD"—"I AM WHO I AM." He "who is the blessed and only Sovereign, the King of kings and Lord of lords, who alone has immortality, who dwells in unapproachable light, whom no one has ever seen or can see" (1 Tim. 6:15–16).

The Lord has these incommunicable attributes—parts of His character that we do not share with Him. Although we are made in His image, there are some aspects of who He is that we cannot and will not replicate. In our folly we may think we can, but wisdom knows we are unable.

He is independent. He doesn't need us nor anything He has made. We are utterly dependent creatures. We need air to breathe—and not just any gas, but a specific element, oxygen. We need food. We need human interaction. Our needs are practically endless.

The Lord is immutable. He does not change. Remember, He is the only one who "always and nevers." Praise His name that we are not immutable! If this were the case, I would always be selfish, self-centered, self-seeking, jealous, envious, discontent, and immature in every way! By His grace, though, He is changing me—conforming me into the image of His beloved Son (Rom. 8:29).

God has no beginning and no end. He is eternal. I am a blip on the radar. Our lives are but a breath. Although we are promised everlasting life if we trust in Him, I know I had a beginning. My mother knows it even better than I do!

He is omnipresent. There's nowhere that He's not. Whether the heights or the depths, He is there (Ps. 139:8). My kids might be the happiest to know that I am, in fact, not everywhere all the time.

The rest of these incommunicable traits are His omnipotence, sovereignty, omniscience, and wisdom, but I want to save room for the last three: His holiness, love, and wrath. There's a scene in Scripture that displays these traits beautifully.

Isaiah was a prophet of the Most High God. Though he was chosen by God, he wasn't exactly loved and admired by the people.

The Lord was gracious to give him a vibrant vision that, I would imagine, provided comfort on darker days.

In Isaiah 6, the prophet details what he saw. It says that he saw the Lord sitting upon His throne, high and lifted up. Didn't 1 Timothy 6:16 say that no one has seen Him? How is this possible? Since both texts are canonized Scripture, I can trust that both are true. So there has to be something else going on here. Isaiah must be seeing a portion of who God is, and 1 Timothy is referring to the whole of who God is. Isaiah is seeing what the Lord has allowed him to see. In particular, He is letting Isaiah see His sovereignty (as He is seated on a throne, high and lifted up) and His holiness. This is confirmed when the angels surrounding Him break into song:

> "Holy, holy, holy is the LORD of hosts;
> the whole earth is full of his glory!" (Isa. 6:3)

Holy is such a churchy word. Nowhere else do we use this adjective except in a religious context (unless we're swearing or expressing disbelief that has something to do with bovines). The ESV Study Bible notes define His holiness this way: "God is absolutely and uniquely excellent above all creation (majesty) and without sin (purity)."[2]

The prophet is acutely aware of this. If it wasn't made evident upon seeing the Lord on His throne, it was punctuated with "the foundations of the thresholds" shaking and the house filling with smoke. This is reminiscent of the Israelites' experience with the Holy God—the flashes of lightning, thunder, sounds of trumpets, and the mountain smoking. That's where the similarity ends though. Isaiah didn't shrink back and say, "Lord, speak to someone else and let them carry the message to me," as Israel did. He exhibited the fear of the Lord instead. He knew he was in the presence of a holy, sovereign God and there was no one more powerful than He. To whom could he run? No, he knew his only hope was to cry out to the Lord.

"Woe is me!" he says, "For I am lost; for I am a man of unclean lips, and I dwell in the midst of a people of unclean lips; for my eyes have seen the King, the LORD of hosts!" (Isa. 6:5).

The sight of God's holiness indicted Isaiah and exposed his inadequacy. Who was he in light of the King, the Lord of hosts? All earthly wisdom was burned up by God's presence. The fear of the Lord sprouted in Isaiah's heart. He beheld God in His holiness, in His perfection, and it laid him open. He knew that he couldn't measure up on his own—nor could anyone else. He was frozen in fear because he knew he was completely powerless to do anything. The beginning of wisdom is coming to the end of ourselves.

PURIFICATION

In His perfect love, God sent forth the seraphim (an angel) to touch his lips with a burning coal. The Lord took the initiative. He drew near first. In this is love, not that we first loved Him, but that He first loved us.

The seraphim said to Isaiah, "Behold, this has touched your lips; your guilt is taken away, and your sin atoned for" (v. 7). Isn't fire a bit harsh? Couldn't the Lord have just taken a baby wipe and cleaned up Isaiah's mouth? From all appearances, it seems like God was going a little overboard.

The degree of purification is indicative of the degree of the impurity. God's wrath burns white-hot against sin because of sin's affront to a holy God. God hates sin and His hate is directly proportional to His love. If He loved little, He would hate little. But because He loves us intensely, His wrath is equally intense. We see this perfectly in Jesus' crucifixion.

Earthly wisdom would have had Jesus coming to teach us how to be good enough. Jesus would have been our life coach equipping us with the tools to do life right. Essentially, He would have said, "You've got this! You just need a little extra help!"

But that's not what happened. Jesus came to die. And it was an ugly, dishonorable death. He was wrongly convicted. Beaten beyond recognition. A bloody, mangled pulp of flesh. He was forced to carry His own cross—at least 100 pounds of splintering wood rubbing against raw wounds with each step and stumble.

When He could finally shed the weight of the cross, He was laid down on it. Roman soldiers held Jesus' arms and legs down, one at a time, driving nails through skin, bones, ligaments, and nerves. Each thud of the hammer sent waves of searing pain throughout Jesus' whole body.

Once they finished nailing Him to the cross, they raised Him up. The bottom post of the cross hit the ground with a thud. Gravity pulled on Jesus' pierced hands and feet with agonizing force. For hours that must have felt like days, Jesus gasped for air. Naked and exposed to the elements, He endured the spiteful jeers of the people as they looked up at Him with contempt. "If You're truly the Son of God," they spat, "come down from that cross!" "Look! He saved others, let Him save Himself!"

Shameful and painful. Hundreds of years before Christ would hang on that cross, Isaiah was given these words about Him:

He was despised and rejected by men;
a man of sorrows, and acquainted with grief;

and as one from whom men hide their faces
he was despised, and we esteemed him not.
Surely he has borne our griefs
and carried our sorrows;
yet we esteemed him stricken,
smitten by God, and afflicted.
But he was pierced for our transgressions;
he was crushed for our iniquities;
upon him was the chastisement that brought us peace,
and with his wounds we are healed. (Isa. 53:3–5)

Jesus' death was harsh and unfair. The punishment far exceeded the crime—so it seemed. Yes, Jesus was absolutely innocent. But we are not. The people who mocked and despised Him were giving voice to what our hearts claim when we set ourselves up in our earthly wisdom. We scoff at the need of a savior. We make light of our sin and thus God's wrath—and His love.

All we like sheep have gone astray;
we have turned—every one—to his own way;
and the Lord has laid on him
the iniquity of us all. (Isa. 53:6)

The Lord did not deal with us according to what we deserve. His wrath was poured out on Christ. It burned hot in every pang of the soldier's hammer.

Yet it was the will of the Lord to crush him;
he has put him to grief;
when his soul makes an offering for guilt,

> *he shall see his offspring; he shall prolong his days;*
> *the will of the* Lord *shall prosper in his hand.*
> *Out of the anguish of his soul he shall see and be satisfied;*
> *by his knowledge shall the righteous one, my servant,*
> *make many to be accounted righteous,*
> *and he shall bear their iniquities.* (Isa. 53:10–11)

Jesus didn't come as our life coach; He came to show us what we could never do on our own. He exposed and uprooted our earthly wisdom and "by his knowledge" He made "many to be accounted righteous."

This is the beginning of wisdom: when we rightly see the Lord in all His majesty and purity, acknowledge our sin against a holy God, and realize there is nowhere to turn but to Him. When the people suffering from their own folly in Psalm 107 did this, it says, "He sent out his word and healed them, and delivered them from their destruction" (v. 20).

A GOOD WORD

God's Word always brings life. It was with a word that He brought forth all creation. The commandments that He spoke to Moses were for the good of His people—that they would live long in the land He promised them. It's not just the Law through which God speaks life, but all of Scripture. Second Timothy 3:16–17 says that "all Scripture is breathed out by God and profitable for teaching, for reproof, for correction, and for training in righteousness, that the man of God may be complete, equipped for every good work."

Becoming wise means not only fearing the Lord, but knowing His Word. The Scriptures are the food that Jesus talked about when He answered Satan's temptation to turn stones into bread. We don't live by physical food alone, but on the "manna and quail" generously provided in God's Word.

The longest chapter in the Bible, Psalm 119, is a love song to God as He is revealed by Scripture. The psalmist croons delight in meditating on Scripture, "Oh how I love your law! It is my meditation all the day" (v. 97).

When Matt and I met, I admit that I was slightly obsessed. But to be fair, so was he! I remember those early days—of young love. Neither one of us could eat much, which brought a whole new meaning to lovesick. Few moments would go by that I wasn't aware of his existence. The more I came to know him, the worse it got. There were new things to think about, new aspects of his person that begged to be admired. Oh, how I loved Matt Chandler! He was my meditation all the day!

Like the psalmist in Psalm 119, I was smitten. The object of my desire, however, was Matt. The psalmist's desire was God's Word. He'd gotten a taste of it and dreamed about every bite from then on. It had proven sweet and sustainable.

In our folly, we stuff ourselves with what may taste sweet at first, but it leaves a bitter aftertaste. And we are always emptier than we were before we indulged. We feed on our own wisdom and it makes us sick. However, when we turn to God, when we cry out to Him, He gives us back our appetite and fills us with good things—namely, His Word.

For over a year now, I have been meeting almost weekly with a group of women. Although we are friends and share our hearts and lives with each other, our main focus is studying the Word of God. Each week we open the Bible and talk about what it says and how that bears on our lives. Some weeks are easier than others; the pages lay before us and truth is easy to discern and apply.

Other times, we either wrestle to understand or struggle to humbly submit to what it says. In addition to mining the Scriptures for gems, we memorize and recite it. It's like 2nd grade Sunday school all over again—but without the stickers. Our reward is having God's Word written on our hearts and minds. Chapters of James and Romans are now tucked away in our brains. It's work but it's worth it.

There's a warning we should heed, though. In John 5, Jesus had just healed a man who had been lame for thirty-eight years. That wouldn't seem like a problem, right? To the Pharisees (the most religious Jews) though, it was an abomination. Jesus had healed the man on the Sabbath. In their eyes, He had broken the Sabbath. The act of healing was not on their list of acceptable practices on what was meant to be a day of rest. They had taken what God had said and twisted it to suit their preferences. The Pharisees missed the whole point. Jesus calls them on it saying, "You search the Scriptures because you think that in them you have eternal life; and it is they that bear witness about me, yet you refuse to come to me that you may have life" (John 5:39–40).

Our healing is only found in Jesus—the Word made flesh. We devour Scripture so that we may know God, that we may see Him and love Him. Folly is to know His Word without knowing Him.

PEACE WITH OTHERS

As folly produces bitterness, jealousy, anger, and selfish ambition, wisdom bears fruit in our lives as well. James 3:17 describes the harvest of wisdom from above: "But the wisdom from above is first pure, then peaceable, gentle, open to reason, full of mercy and good fruits, impartial and sincere."

Godly wisdom in itself is pure. It's not mixed with anything of a "different, inferior or contaminating kind."[3] It is always for God's glory and our good. There are no ulterior motives. Wisdom from above knows that since God is "the only Sovereign," He is the only One worthy of glory.

He alone can bear the weight of the world and the weight of our worship. We see this played out sadly in the realm of celebrity life. Few of the famous are able to sustain the burden of fame. They turn to drugs, false religions, or are forced into hiding. They shave their heads, act out rebelliously, or even take their own lives. Humans were not meant to shoulder stardom. As the moon reflects the light of the sun, so are we meant to reflect the glory of God.

This is a load off our shoulders. And a burden lifted is a good thing. The purity of wisdom leads to peace—peace within ourselves and peace with others. There's no striving to be the point of life so there's a rest for our souls. Likewise, we no longer have to live at odds with others. When I operate as if I'm the point, others are seen as threats to my goal in life. They are simply problems I have to manage rather than people I get to serve.

Wisdom affords me the opportunity to love peace with others by humbling myself and counting others as more important. I can look not only to my own interests but also to the interests of others, keeping in mind that:

Though [Christ] was in the form of God, did not count equality with God a thing to be grasped, but emptied himself, by taking the form of a servant, being born in the likeness of men. And being found in human form, he humbled himself by becoming obedient to the point of death, even death on a cross. (Phil. 2:6–8)

Jesus became my peace with God so that I could live in peace with others. This allows me to respond to others in gentleness because I have been dealt with so gently. Jesus issues an invitation in Matthew 11:29, "Take my yoke upon you, and learn from me, for I am gentle and lowly in heart, and you will find rest for your souls." He bears with us. He doesn't look down on us struggling beneath the weight of life and say, "You need to lift with your legs a little more . . . no, not like that!"

In the same way, we are freed up to bear with others. The apostle Paul exhorts us in Romans 15:1–2, "We who are strong have an obligation to bear with the failings of the weak, and not to please ourselves. Let each of us please his neighbor for his good, to build him up." We enter into the lives of those around us. We get our hands dirty, so to speak. Godly wisdom lets us remember that on our own we are weak and only by God's grace are we given strength to endure. And that strength isn't meant for us alone but for the good of others.

This is good news. We won't always be the strong ones. There will be days when we need someone to remind us of what it means to fear the Lord—to trust Him even when we have a hard time seeing Him. We will need a friend who will bear our burden with us.

Friendship is a gift from the Lord. Not only does it provide a soft place to land, but it grants us others' eyes to see what we cannot. Godly wisdom is open to reason. We recognize that we don't know everything, only God is omniscient. Thus, we are in need of a community that is willing to say the hard things, and our hearts must be open to receiving it.

My bent toward perfectionism can hinder my willingness to be "open to reason." To be open to hearing how I might be doing something wrong, or not the most efficient way, rubs against the grain of my folly. I had a dear, loving friend who sat me down to tenderly bring to my attention an area of neglect. She is a brave soul who valued my good more than she valued her standing with me.

There are a few areas of life that are treacherous to navigate in friendship. Two of which are parenting and marriage. From the outside we may see habits as parents that don't serve one's children well, or interactions with spouses that don't serve them well either. Once we breach the subject, there's no turning back, no "un-saying" of what was said.

My friend brought up an aspect of my parenting that cut me to the heart. I hadn't seen the unhealthy pattern on my own so my defenses went up immediately. I was prickly with my friend at the end of our conversation and unsure of what to do with the information. As the day wore on, I was able to see and receive what she put before me. I had to swallow my pride, forsake my veneer of perfection, and repent of my idolatry of comfort. This woman is still a dear friend (if not dearer now!) who has the space to speak into my life. Being open to reason helped me be a better parent and a better friend.

Bearing with one another also means we are "full of mercy and good fruits." We are not only hearers of the Word but doers. The wisdom of God becomes evident in our lives by how we live them. Hoarding isn't an option for those who know that God owns everything and graciously loans us what we have. Open-handed living and generous giving marks those who are wise. Their giving is also impartial and sincere. The station of the person to whom they give is not taken into account. They no longer regard others according to the flesh—if and how those to whom they give can reciprocate—but according to how God has dealt with them in grace and mercy, knowing there's no way we can pay Him back.

They do so honestly, not for appearance's sake, because they know there is One who sees and knows.

Who is wise and understanding? May we be counted among them. May a holy fear of the Lord lead us to lives that are free, open, and generous. May we anchor our souls in the One whom the Scriptures reveal—in His steadfast love, not in our earthly wisdom—so that we may be immovable in the midst of the storm.

PART FIVE

The Storm

Some went down to the sea in ships,
doing business on the great waters;
they saw the deeds of the LORD,
his wondrous works in the deep.
For he commanded and raised the stormy wind,
which lifted up the waves of the sea.
They mounted up to heaven; they went down to the depths;
their courage melted away in their evil plight;
they reeled and staggered like drunken men
and were at their wits' end.
Then they cried to the LORD in their trouble,
and he delivered them from their distress.
He made the storm be still,
and the waves of the sea were hushed.
Then they were glad that the waters were quiet,
and he brought them to their desired haven.

Let them thank the Lord for his steadfast love,
for his wondrous works to the children of man!
Let them extol him in the congregation of the people,
and praise him in the assembly of the elders.
He turns rivers into a desert, springs of water into thirsty ground,
a fruitful land into a salty waste, because of the evil of its inhabitants.
He turns a desert into pools of water, a parched land into springs of water.
And there he lets the hungry dwell, and they establish a city to live in;
they sow fields and plant vineyards and get a fruitful yield.
By his blessing they multiply greatly,
and he does not let their livestock diminish.
When they are diminished and brought low
through oppression, evil, and sorrow,
he pours contempt on princes
and makes them wander in trackless wastes;
but he raises up the needy out of affliction
and makes their families like flocks.
The upright see it and are glad,
and all wickedness shuts its mouth.
Whoever is wise, let him attend to these things;
let them consider the steadfast love of the Lord.

⚓

CHAPTER TEN

At Sea

When I was fifteen, Glo died. She was everything warm, bright, and adventurous to me. Born with a feeble heart, she was bedridden for years as a child. All her days spent lying in bed only served as a chance to dream about all the things she would do outside of it. She stored up decades of missed exploits and spent them generously the rest of her years with her husband, daughter, and two sons (the youngest being my father).

The day her heart finally gave out, I surveyed every square inch of her dwelling. Any artifact I could find, any treasure to tuck away. On her refrigerator door hung a calendar. Her perfectly slanted cursive marked appointments, reminders, and outings. Struck with sadness, I realized she would never have the chance to stick to her schedule.

A storm overtakes us like that. We make plans. We pen appointments. But we're never guaranteed to have it turn out like we think it will.

Proverbs 16:9 says, "The heart of a man plans his way, but the LORD establishes his steps."

Jeremiah records the Lord's diagnosis of the human heart. He tells us that it's sick, that it deceives us (Jer. 17:9). We think we know what we want, what we need. We think that what we have planned will squeeze the greatest amount of joy from our lives. But the Lord knows what's best. He is what's best. So that storm that seems so inconvenient, so intrusive, so destructive might very well be the Lord establishing something longer lasting, more fulfilling than what your heart could conceive.

Just like the men on the ships in Psalm 107, the storms are an occupational hazard. It's simply part of walking the earth on this side of heaven. Since Adam and Eve's costly bite of fruit, humanity and all creation have suffered the consequences. Strife, struggle, and senseless pain plague us. The storms will come. Would we be willing to have eyes to see "the deeds of the LORD, his wondrous works in the deep" (Ps. 107:24)?

WONDROUS WORKS

When I first read these verses in Psalm 107, I pictured men on large ships peering over the sides at the fauna of the sea—oohing and ahhing at the creatures unlike anything on land. These were the deeds and wondrous works of the Lord that I imagined them seeing. But the more I researched, the more I realized this wasn't the case. Their ships were less like cruise liners and more like glorified sailboats. Although they were likely awed by God's creative work reflected in marine life, it was God's power exhibited in a storm at sea that astounded them most—the waves and wind crashing against their relatively minuscule boat.

At this moment, my laptop is perched on my lap as the beeping and bubbling sounds of a hospital room surround me. My beloved Daddy had triple bypass surgery only a few days ago. His heart is much like his momma's—inside a body that doesn't match his strength—a weak heart, a strong body. Only hours before a trip to the ER, he was texturing and painting the walls of my brother's new home. The Lord pressed the pause button for him, and graciously spared his life. A blockage in the artery nicknamed "the widowmaker" (can't you feel the warm fuzzies?) was detected by tests run in the emergency room. His doctors scheduled bypass surgery for him immediately.

The routine procedure became anything but. Seconds before the surgeon was to wire him shut and determine him fixed, his vitals tanked. Every number on every screen dropped. Puzzled and alarmed, the surgeon went back in to find the culprit—a clot that blocked the flow of blood through his heart. If that clot had lodged any later, there's a good chance that I wouldn't be sitting in this recovery room. I would be sitting in a funeral home helping my mom make decisions she wished she didn't have to make.

The night of his surgery, with the weight of what almost happened on my shoulders, I drove home from the hospital watching the sky. Lightning etched veins in the clouds. Thunder pounded the earth. I was riveted by the glorious display of God's majesty.

Why would He consider me or my dad? I thought. *Tiny flecks of flesh on a big blue ball in space. Why would He use all that power to save Daddy's life?*

I lifted my voice through tears and thanked Him. I blessed Him for considering me, my dad, my mom, my brother, my family. He let me see His wondrous works in the storm. He didn't have to intervene, but I'm glad He did. I know He would have shown His power in sustaining us in the loss as much as He showed it in sustaining Daddy's life.

HE COMMANDED

It's a comfort to know that God is Lord over the storm. The psalmist attributes the activity of the wind and waves to God.

We see an account of His mastery through the Son in Mark 4:35–41:

On that day, when evening had come, he said to them, "Let us go across to the other side." And leaving the crowd, they took him with them in the boat, just as he was. And other boats were with him. And a great windstorm arose, and the waves were breaking into the boat, so that the boat was already filling. But he was in the stern, asleep on the cushion. And they woke him and said to him, "Teacher, do you not care that we are perishing?" And he awoke and rebuked the wind and said to the sea, "Peace! Be still!" And the wind ceased, and there was a great calm. He said to them, "Why are you so afraid? Have you still no faith?" And they were filled with great fear and said to one another, "Who then is this, that even the wind and the sea obey him?"

Jesus had been teaching large crowds beside the sea. His disciples were with Him there as well. They listened to Him speak in parables to the people and leaned in when He gathered them around and explained the stories' meanings. The disciples had backstage access to the unparalleled Teacher. They didn't have to wonder what He meant by the "seeds falling on rocky soil." They were close enough to ask Him about it. He unfolded the mystery for them and then, unbeknownst to them, provided an opportunity to take what they knew in their heads and make it real in their hearts.

He does that. He loves us too much to let the knowledge puff up. He invites us to let it sink in deep—beyond skin deep. Most often, I've noticed, He uses the adversity of the storm more than the advantage of the calm. Not because He's cruel, but because

I'm hard-headed. And, I have a hard time hearing His voice over the lullaby of prosperity. So He takes me by the hand and leads me to a place where I can hear Him better.

It was Jesus' idea to set foot on the boat that would take them to the other side. The phrase "let us" is repeated countless times in the Old and New Testament. Most often it precedes an act of the will—man's will or God's will—depending on who is saying it. The first time we see the phrase in Scripture is when God created man. He says, "Let us make man in our image, after our likeness" (Gen. 1:26). The next time the phrase is uttered in Scripture, it's the builders of the Tower of Babel who use it. Dissatisfied with making much of their Creator, they exert their desire and will to "make a name for [themselves]" (Gen. 11:4). *Let us make man in our image*—God's will. *Let us make a name for ourselves*—man's will. Also to note is the fact that God accomplished His "let us" while the Babel builders never had the chance to finish their task.

So when Jesus says, "Let us go across to the other side," we can count on two things: it's the will of God and it will be accomplished. That's why He was able to fall asleep in the stern. He knew what was coming and He knew how He would handle it.

We don't have that luxury—neither did the disciples. Some had experience on the Sea of Galilee: Andrew, Peter, James, and John had been called from their lives as fishermen to become "fishers of men." A trip across the sea wasn't a new thing for them. They were familiar with the sea but not comfortably so. More than likely, they knew to expect the unexpected. The Sea of Galilee, the lowest freshwater lake on the earth, is positioned 696 feet below sea level just south of Mt. Hermon. The downdraft from such great heights (Mt. Hermon) to such great depths (the Sea of Galilee) stirs up all kinds of trouble at sea. Stepping onto the boat, they knew there was an element of risk.

As readers on this side of their story, we could ask, "Couldn't they have been at ease knowing they were going aboard with God in the flesh?" At this point, they weren't really sure who He was. Yes, He was a teacher like they'd never heard and was able to work signs and wonders, but was He a prophet like Elijah or something else?

It was in the storm that they began to grapple with who Jesus really was. It was in the storm that He became more than a good teacher, more than a movement leader, but what He was—what He is—was still not fully known to them. But they got a glimpse.

Their boat was already taking on water when they finally woke Jesus. Can you imagine the ruckus? The seasoned fishermen shouting at each other, securing sails, bailing water, and Jesus sawing logs in the back of the boat (He was a carpenter, after all)? I can picture Peter wrestling with ropes and flabbergasted by Jesus' nap.

How can He sleep at a time like this? Doesn't He even care that we are going to die?

God can come off that way in the midst of the storm, can't He? When we're reeling from the wind and the waves, it sure can feel like God is taking a nap. I can find myself asking Him, *Do You even care about me, about what I'm going through?* In the vast sea, it can seem reasonable that He doesn't—why should He? We are but a speck in the endless ocean!

We see that He does, in fact, care. Although the disciples could have used the rebuking, Jesus instead reprimanded the wind and waves. He spoke as a superior to an inferior, like a parent to a child: "Stop it and be quiet." And they did. It says the wind ceased. It didn't die down, it stopped completely. The waves went from liquid mountains to glassy calm in an instant. The same power that "raises the stormy wind" and "lifts up the waves of the sea" is the same power that "makes the storm be still" and "hushes the waves of the sea."

Then Jesus turned to His disciples and asked them a question. As we've seen, when Jesus asks a question, it's not to gather information. It's to make something clear to the one whom He asks.

"Why are you so afraid? Have you still no faith?"

The account of this story in Luke 8 has Jesus asking them this question: "Where is your faith?"

Location, not existence, becomes the issue. They're putting their faith somewhere; it's just not where it should be. Their faith is in the power of the storm—the wind that knocks them off their feet and the waves that threaten to drown. I don't fault them for putting their faith there—for believing the storm will overcome them. When we're in the storm, the wind and the waves feel real.

The diagnosis

The prognosis

The anxiety

The unknowns

The bills piling high

The job loss

The empty crib

The death of a loved one—those things feel real. Those things we can taste, touch, hear, smell, and see. They demand attention. C. S. Lewis once wrote:

We can ignore even our pleasure. But our pain insists upon being attended to. God whispers to us in our pleasures, speaks in our conscience, but shouts in our pain: it is His megaphone to rouse a deaf world.[1]

The pain inflicted by the storm is God's grace to help us quit trusting in our circumstances—whether the good or the bad. It peels back the veil from our eyes. Before the storm, we are easily fooled into thinking that we have something to do with our well-being, or that having certain things in our lives ensures stability. But when we're eyeball to eyeball with the wind and the waves, we quickly see through the veneer. We come to our "wit's end" just like the men in the ships in Psalm 107. We reel, we stagger, our courage melts. We come to the end of ourselves and discover there's only one anchor for our soul—only One who is able to manage the unmanageable storm.

"Still he seeks the fellowship of his people and sends them both sorrows and joys in order to detach their love from other things and attach it to himself."[2] If all our hope is tied to what cannot sustain, wouldn't it be God's wrath to let us stay tethered to the false anchors? So when we ask Him in the midst of the storm, "Do You even care?" We can be confident that He replies with a resounding "YES." If He didn't care, we wouldn't be where we are. We would be floating along merrily, oblivious to our peril.

JONAH

Dr. Timothy Keller, in his sermon on Mark 4:35–41, draws his listeners' attention to how the gospel writer parallels the telling of this account of trouble at sea to Jonah's. God gave Jonah the task to go to Nineveh and "call out against it." In modern words, "to call them out" on their sin. Jonah resisted by fleeing to Tarshish. To get to Tarshish, he had to hitch a ride on a ship launching from Joppa.

Once on the boat, Scripture says "the LORD hurled a great wind upon the sea, and there was a mighty tempest on the sea, so that the ship threatened to break up" (Jonah 1:4). The pagan sailors broke into a frenzy, throwing cargo overboard and crying out to any god that came to mind. Guess where Jonah was. He was in the inner part of the ship sleeping. Sound familiar?

The captain scolded him incredulously, "What do you mean, you sleeper? Arise, call out to your god!" (v. 6).

Jonah knew all along that it was because of his disobedience that they were suffering the storm. But he didn't let on. He waited for them to cast lots before he said a word. When the lot fell to Jonah, he finally admitted that he was running from the presence of his God—the Lord, maker of sea and dry land. The mariners knew their suffering was because of Jonah, so they pressed him. They asked him what they should do. Jonah responded in his first selfless moment, "Hurl me into the sea."

These men who had never known the Lord hesitated to do such a thing. They rowed hard and tried to make it through the tempest without drowning Jonah. They didn't want his blood on their hands. But when it became evident there would be no deliverance in their own power, they cried out to the Lord, "O LORD, let us not perish for this man's life, and lay not on us innocent blood, for you, O LORD, have done as it pleased you" (Jonah 1:14). So they picked Jonah up and threw him into the sea.

God did not forsake Jonah even in his disobedience. He appointed a large fish to swallow him and preserve his life. Three days and three nights later, Jonah got a "do-over." He set his face toward Nineveh to make them aware of the impending destruction as a result of their wickedness. Much to Jonah's self-righteous displeasure, they repented. God, in His mercy, spared the city.

WHY NOT US?

These are two accounts of God's power over the storm, His mercy through the storm, and His deliverance from the storm. If we're willing to look closely and reason candidly, we can see ourselves in both.

We are the sailors. We go about our days oblivious to the maker of the sea and dry land. When trouble arises, we pull out our gods and look to them for relief and deliverance. We escape to fantasies, comforts, addictions, habits, even our good works done in our good name. All our means of gaining control over our lives fall short. At our wits' end, we cry out to the Lord.

We are Jonah. God has called us to walk in obedience because that's where we will only find lasting joy. And yet, we refuse. It's too hard. *You've got the wrong person, God,* we say. Our disobedience catches up with us and God sends a storm to wake us up. We suffer the consequences and resign ourselves to a watery grave—a hopeless end fitting our rebellion. But before our toes sink in the sandy bottom, deliverance comes in the most unexpected form. The storm threatened to swallow us up but God made a way in the depths.

Some of the most beautiful stories of redemption have happened when people have hit rock bottom. They knowingly ran from God, and He chose a storm for their deliverance. Just when they thought they were suffering their "just desserts," sinking into oblivion, they looked up and saw God to the rescue. "They cried out to the LORD and he delivered them from their distress."

We are the disciples. We've left everything to follow Christ. We've counted the cost of losing our life to find it in Him. We trust Him. We've stepped into the boat—at His prompting—to go to the other side. We didn't ask for a storm. This wasn't supposed to be part of the deal. Why us?

Why not us?

There's a lie that has crept into the North American church: saying yes to Christ means we've said no to the storm. But here we see that there are times Christ leads us into the storm. Like the disciples, we listen to (or in our case, read) Jesus' parable of the sower. How the seed that falls on the path is snatched up by birds, the seed on rocky ground springs up quickly and withers, the seed in the thorns is choked out and produces no grain, and the seed on good soil grows and produces an abundant crop. Surely, we tell ourselves, *we are the good soil. Our hearts receive the word with joy!* Oh, but our hearts are prone to deceive us. We don't know the true condition of our hearts until we are tested. Sometimes the Lord chooses to use the storm to reveal the truth. The wind and waves lay us bare, and Christ comes in to be the better Jonah.

ATONEMENT

Like Jonah, Jesus had a message from the Father to deliver to sinful people:

> *For God so loved the world, that he gave his only Son, that whoever believes in him should not perish but have eternal life. For God did not send his Son into the world to condemn the world, but in order that the world might be saved through him. Whoever believes in him is not condemned, but whoever does not believe is condemned already, because he has not believed in the name of the only Son of God.* (John 3:16–18)

Unlike Jonah, Christ didn't shirk His responsibility. He "humbled himself by becoming obedient to the point of death, even death on a cross" (Phil. 2:8). Like Jonah, Jesus was found sleeping in the stern while the storm raged. Unlike Jonah, Jesus had the power to deliver them from it. Jesus doesn't just deliver us from the storm at sea but the storm that threatens to obliterate us all—the power of sin and death. As Jonah offered himself as a sacrifice to save the rest of the ship, so Jesus offered himself as a sacrifice to save those who would trust in Him. He weathered the worst storm for us to show how much He loves us.

In weathering the storm of sin and death, He had to face the storms of the human experience. He had to become fully human although He remained fully God. He suffered the loss of a friend (John 11:35). He had "nowhere to lay his head" (Matt. 8:20). He was oppressed and afflicted (Isa. 53:7). In the words of Melissa Moore, "He knows it's scary to be us."[3] His knowledge is firsthand and intimate. "For we do not have a high priest who is unable to sympathize with our weaknesses, but one who in every respect has been tempted as we are, yet without sin" (Heb. 4:15). His faith never wavered. He knew who He was and what He was sent to do.

Remember the sailors' words in the story of Jonah—"O Lord, let us not perish for this man's life, and lay not on us innocent blood, for you, O Lord, have done as it pleased you." For the Christian, our plea is different. There is no deliverance unless innocent blood is laid on us. We plead the blood of Christ. For "he entered once for all into the holy places, not by means of the blood of goats and calves but by means of his own blood, thus securing an eternal redemption" (Heb. 9:12).

The Mosaic Law required a blood sacrifice for the atonement of sin. The blood of a goat and a bull was sprinkled on the altar to atone for the sins of the priest and the people. Jesus offered His own blood—pure and innocent—for the sins of the people. He didn't have to make an offering for His sin because He was sinless.

And He doesn't have to make it over and over again. Once and for all, His blood speaks a better word—eternal redemption. It cries out, covered! Saved!

The storm of the power of sin and death can only be calmed by admitting that Christ "threw himself overboard" to atone for our sin. We have no hope for rescue and redemption unless His blood covers us. Comfort is found in knowing our sins are not counted against us, and that the One who leads us into the boat to reach the other side will get us there.

The storm is scary. It tests our faith and reveals the true condition of our hearts. But I wouldn't trade the seasons in the storm for anything else. Just as the disciples began to have an inkling of who Jesus was when He calmed the wind and the waves, and just as they were invited to let head knowledge take root in their hearts, so I came to more fully know Jesus in the midst of the storm.

CHAPTER ELEVEN

Our Storm

That Thursday morning, I actually had my act together. Somewhat. Fully dressed and armed for the day, I shuffled into the closest grocery store open on a holiday morning. Only a few items were absentmindedly left off the shopping list from the multiple trips the previous day. I exhaled a sigh of relief while at the same time graciously accepted my own pat on the back as I gathered each one and neared the checkout line in record time. Glossy pages of Christmas feast perfection teased contentment and ease. Yeah right. And I was struggling to piece a few dishes together for Thanksgiving!

Creeping back into our house through the garage door, I could tell by the sounds coming from the living room that stealth-mode was in vain. Everyone was awake clamoring for breakfast. Luckily, the fulfillment of their desire was packed away in a bag just ready to be unwrapped, dented with a spoon and (Christianly) cursed as it opened with a jack-in-the-box pop.

The cinnamon rolls were cooling on the baking sheet, the side dishes were coming along swimmingly and all seemed right with the world. A crash from the next room shattered the fragile peace. It wasn't just the peace of the moment; it was the peace of my existence. You see, I always assumed life would progress according to my best-laid plan. Marriage would give way to childbearing; childbearing would usher in a couple of decades of sleepless nights, math homework, slamming doors, and heartfelt conversations at bedtime. And those decades would simmer to a slow-boiling empty nest—until grandchildren broke the monotony. All would be seasoned with ministry pursuits.

The morning of Thanksgiving 2009 changed my perspective forever. The tumult from the living room piqued my curiosity. I knew my husband Matt was there with our three children. Why was there no explanation for the racket? I expected to hear, "It's okay, honey!" Instead, silence. Finally, my then six-year-old Audrey called out with confusion, "Daddy?"

Walking into the room, I spotted my four-year-old watching cartoons, my six-month-old bouncing in her Johnny Jump Up and Audrey gazing at the space between our coffee table and the fireplace ledge. That narrow distance cradled my precious, strong husband in the most vulnerable position of his life. His body shook with force. As much as he comes across as being self-controlled and competent, in that moment, he was as defenseless and weak as a newborn.

Dropping to my knees I shielded his thrashing from our children. I yelled for my phone and Audrey supplied it. My voice was calm, collected, everything I wasn't on the inside. The fire station was so close I could hear the sirens as the ambulance started toward our home. Home. The last place one imagines seeing emergency vehicles parked in front.

Medics rolled in with their stretcher and black bulky bags. Matt's body had finally eased into a deep, sleep-like trance. Vitals were taken, basic inquiries made, answers (to the best of my knowledge) given. The personnel were kind and even gentle as they asked me where I wanted them to take him.

"Lewisville."

Hoisting myself into the front seat of the ambulance, I began to wonder.

Is this the rest of my life? Will I take care of a man who is but a shadow of whom he used to be? Did his brain forever break?

EVEN IF HE DOESN'T

There's a story in the Bible that I've heard Matt preach more times than I can recall. Three men bold enough to trust in the power and faithfulness of God while the heat of a fiery furnace drew sweat from their brows more than fear pushed it from their palms. They defied the king's decree. They would not bend a knee to the cheap imitation of the One True God. A price had to be paid for such an affront. The king, incensed, warned them that they would face the fire if they did not bow the knee. The next words out of their mouths were what I begged my heart to repeat with earnest, "If this be so, our God whom we serve is able to deliver us from the burning fiery furnace, and he will deliver us out of your hand, O king. But if not, be it known to you, O king, that we will not serve your gods or worship the golden image that you have set up" (Dan. 3:17–18).

If this be so.

Our God is able.

He will deliver.

And even if He doesn't.

If it be so that my faith and my family would be inserted into the fiery trial of an incapacitated husband and father.

Our God is able to heal my husband completely.

He will deliver us from the hand of the enemy, from the hand of fear.

And even if He doesn't deliver us without singe, even if the flames lick until faith is charred thin, yet would I trust in Him and Him alone.

Even in the fiery furnace He would go with me. In all the sad and hard scenarios my mind could conceive, He would be there.

I needed Him in the very next moment. My thoughts were arrested by the clamor behind me. A gruff voice urged, "We're here to help you, sir; please calm down!"

In the back of the truck, a tangle of paramedics and medical paraphernalia and at its center, Matt. Instinctively, I approached Matt's side and did my best to soothe him, to help him understand what was happening. The eyes I had seen myself in so many times were vacant. Not even a hint of recognition. A stab to the heart.

A sobering yet comforting realization formed within me. Even if he never remembered who I was, what we had shared, the life we knew together, I knew I would love him. I knew a love bigger than I could manage on my own would pour through me. There would be this steadfast love that would carry me even in the hard days.

Once the paramedics won the scuffle, the drugs they had administered took effect. The white of Matt's knuckles released pink, his breaths lengthened. We were finally on our way to the hospital.

"Hey, honey! What happened?"

A songbird couldn't have sounded sweeter.

"Baby, you had a seizure."

"Really? I am so sorry!"

Seriously? He's sorry? What on earth could he have done about it?

My heart broke over his tenderness and care for me and his children despite his fragile state. They wheeled him into a small room. Tests were ordered, scans scheduled. As soon as Matt was barely able to make sense of what was happening, he found himself in a CT machine. Shortly after, an MRI tube.

Friends and family encircled us as the ER doctor solemnly delivered the news. An unidentified mass. Right frontal lobe. A neurosurgeon should be contacted as soon as possible.

In that moment, we were just relieved to be discharged from the hospital, to be able to go home and try to piece together what was left of the holiday. The plates of turkey, dressing, and other sides weren't as satisfying as they were the years prior. There just wasn't enough salt to save it.

That day, Thanksgiving became more than food to us. It became an occasion to say in our hearts, even if He doesn't let life play out how we planned, we would give thanks for His deliverance, no matter the form in which it comes. And we would give thanks that He was there with us, that He would continue to be with us.

WHAT IF

Days later, we sat in the neurosurgeon's office. He gathered us around his desktop. The screen revealed what had been hidden in Matt's skull for an unknown amount of time. This intruder, how long had it tagged along? How many occasions did it attend uninvited? To Matt's and my untrained eye, it became evident that this was something that could not be overlooked.

Dr. Barnett pointed out the jagged borders, the fingers of cells gone rogue.

"This must come out. I've made room in my schedule for surgery on Friday."

It was Tuesday.

I soaked up Dr. Barnett's recommendations and next steps. Downstairs to get another scan immediately. Fill out paperwork. More labs. Instructions for pre-surgery.

The list distracted me from the fear that was overtaking Matt, paralyzing him where he sat. In a daze, he nodded at the surgeon, looked toward me asking with his eyes if this was a dream, a very bad dream. I assured him that this was the right decision. I couldn't put into words why I thought that, but either way I was convinced.

His fear was less about losing his life and more about leaving his children with contempt for the God he so desperately loved. He struggled imagining Audrey, Reid, and Norah fatherless and unwilling to look to the heavenly Father, since He had taken their earthly one.

The rest of the day was a blur of phone calls and forms to fill, tears and prayers. Who would take over Matt's responsibilities at church? How, to whom, and in what order should we break the news? What about the kids?

Our community, the dear ones with whom we shared life, rallied around us. They shouldered the burden with us, practically, spiritually, and emotionally. They freed us to spend less time belaboring details and more time with our family.

The days leading up to the surgery are still hard to make out. I can still remember the nights. Almost every time I shut my eyes to sleep, my mind played the tape of Matt's seizure. Fear lurked into our room and whispered the possibility of it happening again as we laid in bed. With prayer and petition, I pushed it back with all my might.

Lord, will this image ever leave my mind? Would You erase it from my memory?

Even in the hotel room the night before the surgery, even after we had been prayed over, after we had lifted our voices together with our friends and family in praise of all the Lord had done and promised to do, that fear nipped. It took advantage of those minutes before my body surrendered to sleep, nudging me with the "what ifs." In God's mercy, He shut its mouth long enough for me to drift off.

It was fitting to wake up the next day to the dark hours of the morning. Just as it was impossible yet to make out the rising sun on the horizon, so it was to see how the day would transpire. There was no knowing how the day would end, but I knew the sun would come.

Matt's phone rang with an expected call. A pastor, tender-hearted and wise, wanted to pray over us. I will not forget his prayer. This man whom Matt and I both admired, from whom we learned the joy of trusting in God's sovereignty, humbly asked the Lord to spare Matt's life.

God delights in our asking. Believing in His sovereignty doesn't mean resigning to "He'll do whatever He wants anyway so why bother?" Believing in His sovereignty means we know that whatever may come our way, it's what is best for us because He knows the future. The future is a place He already is.

Wayne Grudem, in his book *Christian Beliefs*, describes God's omniscience, His all-knowingness, this way:

Since he fully knows himself (1 Cor. 2:10–11), he fully knows all things that he could have done but did not do and all things that he might have created but did not create. He also knows all possible events that will not actually happen, and events that would have resulted if some other events had turned out differently in history (see, for example, Matt. 11:21).[1]

Pastor and author Tim Keller marries God's sovereignty, omniscience, and the prayers of the saints in a way our human minds can grasp: "God will only give you what you would have asked for if you knew everything He knows."[2]

So we ask and believe. We ask for the healing. We ask for the miracle. We ask knowing He is entirely capable. We ask knowing He is the only one who can actually make it happen. We believe that He knows every trajectory of every answer. We believe He is good and will act accordingly. We believe He has our good at heart and will do us no eternal harm if we trust Him.

NOWHERE ELSE TO TURN

On that early morning of one of the most perilous days of my life, I asked the Lord to preserve Matt's life, his voice, his mind, and believed that no matter what the outcome, the Lord would still be good. Our little community met us at the hospital with coffee and doughnuts, hugs and copious amounts of love. Although one cannot weather a storm for another, we can buoy our friends, our brothers and sisters, with prayer, encouragement from Scripture, and the ministry of presence. We can be there for them. Ours were there for us.

Still, there are places we must walk alone. Only I was allowed to go back with Matt to be prepped for surgery. Walled in with privacy curtains, we sang and prayed, trusted and hoped in the Lord together until the nurse and doctors rolled him away. Both of us had our own path into the unknown. Would Matt make it out of surgery? If he did, would he be the same? Would I walk in the hospital as a wife and leave as a widow? Would Matt even remember me or the kids?

God never promises an easy life. In fact, He is pretty clear that the storms will come. As Jesus neared His time to be betrayed, arrested, and crucified, He spoke to His disciples, "In the world you will have tribulation. But take heart; I have overcome the world" (John 16:33). He didn't say "you might" or "*if* you have tribulation." Strongly and clearly He told those whom He loved, "Life will be hard, and the storms will come." And then that glorious conjunction—"but" take heart. Why? Because He has overcome the world. He is the Lord over the storm and the Lord with us in the storm. So although I walked out of the surgery prep room alone, God did not leave me on my own. He was with me.

The waiting room buzzed with family and friends. The pastor of a church nearly a thousand miles away had arranged for lunch to be provided. My Facebook and Twitter feeds exploded with prayers and notes of encouragement. I felt carried on the shoulders of many whom I may never meet. Social media has a dark side, there's no doubt, but it is a venue for just as much, if not more, good.

A nurse called every hour or so to update on Matt's progress. Eight hours after they made the first cut, she told me that he was finally in the neuro-ICU recovering. Shortly after the nurse's call, Dr. Barnett appeared and led us to Matt's room. The pit in my stomach was the size of the Grand Canyon. One fear was allayed: Matt survived the surgery. But another fear vexed: would the blank stare I saw in the ambulance be the same look on his face in the ICU?

To my relief, Matt greeted Dr. Barnett and me with his usual, "Heyy!" He correctly answered the doctor's questions about where he was, who he was, what he'd gone through, and who we were.

I held his hand and looked into his eyes to see if I could still spot "Matt." He was there. He even cracked jokes so that everyone in the room would feel at ease.

The eight-hour trauma to his brain caused his eyes to quiver. His head was wrapped in bandages; and his face was swollen from the intravenous fluids and medication. My rock, once again, was as fragile as I'd ever seen him. I stood at his bedside utterly divided. All at once, I felt two forces pulling me in two different directions. One, to dart into the hallway and weep; while the other pinned me to the floor where I stood. I wanted to be strong for him as he had been strong for me. I didn't want him to see me gasping for air between sobs. In the moment, I thought I was in shock at the sight of him. As I look back, I wonder if all the weight of the week leading up to the surgery, the unknown outcome and implications, and, finally, the relief of seeing him alive, broke the dam of emotion. I'm not easily given to tears but when they come, grab a life raft.

Over the following weeks, Matt got worse before he got better. The medication fog didn't help, but the deficits caused by having a golf-ball-sized piece of his brain removed began to show. His signature facial expressions and warmth faded to a flat affect. The whole left side of his body was weak. The only stimulus he could endure for any length of time was music. One rarely saw him without his ear buds and iPod. I was glad that something brought him comfort but the music began to isolate him from the outside world. Once he recovered his physical strength and some mental clarity, I gently confronted him about it. I entreated him to be present with us, and he conceded.

Hands down, for me the hardest part of this phase of Matt's battle was carrying his diagnosis and prognosis for a week before he was told. Dr. Barnett wanted to divulge the results to me so that we could get moving toward treatment. We waited to tell Matt so that he would have the mental space to heal physically. We didn't want to burden and possibly hinder his recovery. Besides the doctor and myself, only one other person knew Matt was diagnosed with a malignant brain tumor and given only two to three years to live.

I remember stepping out of the hospital conference room in shock. My parents, Matt's parents and sisters, and our close friends searched my face for answers. I don't remember what I told them, if anything. I just remember not wanting to tell others before Matt knew himself. I didn't want everyone having to hold it together for him. And, I felt it was honoring to him to tell him first.

It was a weight worth carrying even if I felt clumsy underneath it. Matt had always been the one to whom I would first go for counsel. To make the decision not to tell anyone else was challenging. I had never really done such a thing. Normally, I would have detailed the situation to Matt, recited my perspective and uncertainties, and then waited to hear his final verdict. But I couldn't this time. I had nowhere else to turn but to the Lord. Sure, I had mentors and godly counselors at my disposal, but I didn't want to reveal the results yet. I felt that I shouldn't. The Lord was faithful to anchor me in His steadfast love. He had been generous in giving me Matt but now He pressed me to press into Him. Like the men in ships, I came to my wits' end. There was no one else to turn to but Him.

THE NEW NORMAL

I was far from perfect in this storm. I was weak. I envied every couple I saw. Hand-holding love birds rubbed salt in my wounds.

Why can't I have that, Lord? Why can't I hold the hand of the man I love without measuring the moments remaining? Why can't I just assume we'll grow old and gray together and not have this prognosis cloud hanging over our heads?

Waves of mourning came at unexpected times. One in particular caught me off guard. After Matt was released from in-patient rehabilitation, he had a week or so of rest before he started eight weeks of low-dose chemo and radiation and then eighteen months of high-dose chemo. For five days a month, Matt took the high-dose chemo in pill form. Each day he grew weaker and more nauseous. All he had the energy for was to lie on the couch and doze off to the television. But our family's world kept spinning—school, homework, diapers, baseball practice, baths, and bedtime stories. Matt rarely had the stamina to attend Reid's baseball practice while he was on chemo. Obviously, I never wanted to put pressure on him to go. I knew he would almost give anything to be there instead of on the sofa. I remember breathlessly juggling a not-yet-one-year-old, seven-year-old and four-year-old and all his baseball paraphernalia to practice one evening. Reid ran off to join his team and I plopped on the grass to entertain the youngest. I glanced around at the other families—the dads supplementing the coach's efforts and the moms looking on from their lawn chairs. Sorrow tightened around my chest, squeezing tears just to the surface. I mourned Matt's absence and entertained the thought that he may never have the opportunity to coach his son in Little League. Were the parents looking at me, wondering where my husband was? Where Reid's father was? Were they filling in the blanks for me? Making assumptions? Did they pity me?

The "new normal" took some adjusting. Everything felt backward. Matt was frail and lacked the strength to anchor our crazy family. I halfway jest that Matt is a better mother than I am! He has such a stabilizing effect on us. I can get a little lost in the weeds while he's able to swoop in with a bird's eye view to make each of us feel heard and loved. Without his clarifying perspective, I struggled to get my feet underneath me. And then I happened upon this verse:

> The LORD is exalted, for he dwells on high;
> he will fill Zion with justice and righteousness,
> and he will be the stability of your times,
> abundance of salvation, wisdom, and knowledge;
> the fear of the LORD is Zion's treasure. (Isa. 33:5–6)

I wept when I read the words in bold. I was "reeling and staggering" (Ps. 107:27). My heart longed for something firm beneath me. I yearned for stability. Here I found comfort: my stability is ultimately found in the Lord. To cry out to Him in the midst of the storm is to find He alone can sustain me.

And He did.

> Then they were glad that the waters were quiet,
> and he brought them to their desired haven. (Ps. 107:30)

Yes, we want the storm to be still. Quiet waters are a welcome sight after the whipping of the wind and waves. But the calm is not enough. We need a safe place to drop anchor—a shelter—a place to catch our breath.

A SAFE HAVEN

As Jesus had a mind to lead the disciples through the storm and to the other side, so the Lord leads us through the storm to a "desired haven." Whether we know it or not, our hearts pine for something in particular. Ecclesiastes 3:11 says that the Lord has put eternity into man's heart. There's a longing in every limited being for the limitless—for something outside ourselves. That Something, or Someone, designed us that way, and He is the only fulfillment of our soul's desire.

He is the object of our desire, and He is our safe haven, or harbor. In order for harbors to be efficient, they must have two important characteristics: depth and protection. The water must be deep enough to allow large ships to drop anchor, and it must be sheltered by prominent land features on several sides from stormy weather. These elements can be found naturally or are constructed artificially by dredging and building seawalls and jettys.

Likewise, when we hide ourselves "in the shelter of the Most High," He provides depth and protection (Ps. 91:1). His love is deep enough to swallow up anyone. No one is too much for Him. And for the curious and knowledge-thirsty, "Oh, the depth of the riches and wisdom and knowledge of God! How unsearchable are his judgments and how inscrutable his ways!" (Rom. 11:33). He is deep enough for our hardest questions—the whys and the why-nots.

We are only safe in Him. A psalm that brought immeasurable comfort in the midst of the storm was Psalm 23:

The LORD is my shepherd; I shall not want.
He makes me lie down in green pastures.
He leads me beside still waters.

He restores my soul.
He leads me in paths of righteousness
for his name's sake.
Even though I walk through the valley of the shadow of death,
I will fear no evil, for you are with me;
your rod and your staff, they comfort me.
You prepare a table before me
in the presence of my enemies;
you anoint my head with oil;
my cup overflows.
Surely goodness and mercy shall follow me
all the days of my life,
and I shall dwell in the house of the LORD forever.

This passage reminds me that although I may walk through the deepest valleys with the darkest shadows, my soul is safe. There is no evil that can overcome me because the Lord is with me. I am comforted by the fact that regardless of what comes my way, whether the loss of my husband, or my children, or reputation, or home, or station in life, it will all be goodness and mercy toward me from the Lord of steadfast love. And one day, I will forever be safe in the house of the Lord.

When I looked for my desired haven in the midst of our storm, I thought what I wanted was Matt's healing and the restoration of the "old normal." While those things are good to desire and even good to petition the Lord for, the healing of one disease can be eclipsed by another dismal diagnosis; and the "old normal" is an infinitely fragile state. No, neither of those can sustain. My desired haven is found in Christ—to be hidden in Him so that when He, who is my life, appears, then also I will appear with Him in glory (Col. 3:4).

The storm reminds me that this is not all there is. There is a glory coming that we have yet to see fully. There is a healing of our souls that goes beyond any physical healing on earth. It's already begun but it's not all here yet. So we wait with eager expectation. We weather the storms with Him on the earth as the wind and waves whet our appetite for the coming glory. Our voices lift from the rain-beaten vessel, "Come, Lord Jesus, come!"

CHAPTER TWELVE

Gratitude

Let them thank the Lord for his steadfast love,
for his wondrous works to the children of man!
Let them extol him in the congregation of the people,
and praise him in the assembly of the elders. (Ps. 107:31–32)

"Did you say, 'thank you'?"

Momma's hand pressed my shoulder, turning me toward the woman standing with us. I turned my face up and momentarily met eyes with her, "Thank you." She smiled, "You're welcome!" I returned the smile and pulled the new doll tightly into my chest.

Why is saying "thank you" so hard for us?

Especially as children, it is a lesson learned, not often a natural response. The older we get and the more we understand the value of things, it becomes easier. But if you're like me, when it comes to the Lord, I can forget to give thanks. This is bad news. Forgetting to thank the Lord is forgetting His will for my life. As Christians, we spend our lives wanting to know, "What is God's will for my life?" We buy books, ask friends and pastors, and take tests designed to help us discover His will for us in particular. Let me help you:

"Rejoice always, pray without ceasing, give thanks in all circumstances; for this is the will of God in Christ Jesus for you" (1 Thess. 5:16–18).

Ta-da!! You're welcome.

What is God's will for you? Rejoice, pray, and give thanks. When? Always, without ceasing, and in all circumstances. We can always rejoice in God's goodness and steadfast love toward us. Joy is a fruit of the Spirit and thus is not dependent upon certain conditions. It is rooted in the imperishable, unchanging, and unconditional. As long as we have the Spirit, we can have eyes to see the Lord's goodness in the land of the living (Ps. 27:13). And in seeing, we can rejoice.

Prayer sharpens our sight. It puts prescriptive lenses on our spiritual eyes. An open line of communication with the Lord allows us to "cry out" in our distress and short-sightedness and to hear and see His response. When I am consciously aware of God's presence and am in conversation with Him all throughout the day, inconveniences become opportunities, disappointments become an occasion to trust the Lord's sovereignty, hurts become a chance to extend the forgiveness extended to me through Christ, fears are overcome by His love for me as His child, and happiness overflows into praise. It's not easy, and it's for sure not natural, but it is essential to the next part of His will for my life: to give thanks in all circumstances.

GRACE

This is where I want to camp for a while—giving thanks. The refrain of Psalm 107 is this: let them thank the Lord for His steadfast love, for His wondrous works to the children of man. Each occurrence of the refrain comes after God's deliverance of the people in distress—after those in the desert are led to a city to dwell in, after the prisoners' bonds are broken, after the foolish are delivered from their own destruction, and after those caught in the storm are brought to their desired haven. Gratitude is a response to God's grace. Karl Barth explains:

Grace and gratitude belong together like heaven and earth. Grace evokes gratitude like the voice of an echo. Gratitude follows grace like thunder lightning. . . . We are speaking of the grace of God who is God for man, and of the gratitude of man as his response to this grace. . . . The two belong together, so that only gratitude can correspond to grace, and this correspondence cannot fail.[1]

When we rejoice always and pray without ceasing, we have eyes with lenses adjusted to count God's grace and respond with its echo—gratitude. Our sight is set on the "God who is God for man," not against man. All circumstances are occasions to identify God's grace toward us and to thank Him for it.

Pregnancy was something my body seemed fitted to do—and not for the obvious reasons. With my first two children, all I had to do was think about wanting a baby and, voilà, two little blue lines confirmed it. Besides a few weeks of fatigue and nausea at night, my pregnancies were textbook. Easy, breezy. The deliveries were just as smooth. So when I finally warmed to the thought of a third child, I consulted our calendar to time the next baby's arrival. If we conceived on this date, the baby would be due around this time. I had it all planned.

Once I was within the time frame for the test to indicate pregnancy, I searched the stick for even the faintest line. I could barely make out a positive result but I reasoned that I was so early on

175

that the hormones hadn't kicked into full gear. I just knew I was pregnant.

Matt, of course, was the first to know, then family and close friends. I dreamed of what we might have—a little brother for Reid or a sister for Audrey. In my family, there's just my younger brother and me, and Matt has two sisters. I grinned at the chance of watching Audrey bond with a sister, and Matt at watching Reid bond with a brother. I imagined all I would eat during the holidays since I had the pregnancy free pass that allows you to indulge without (too much) regret or judgmental looks from others.

Our dreams were short-lived. Before we even heard the heartbeat, I miscarried. I didn't know you could grieve something that never happened, experiences you never had the chance to live. I mourned the loss of the dreams. There would be no baby in July. No free pass during the holidays. No brother or sister for Audrey and Reid.

I had never considered that becoming pregnant is a miraculous gift. It came easy to me. There was little struggle in the process. But after the loss? I gained the appreciation I lacked. I thanked God that He blessed me with Audrey and Reid. My eyes were adjusted through the loss to see the grace He had already granted to me through them. Gratitude followed grace.

We took a break from "trying." The loss was barely a speed bump on the road to becoming a family of five. Three short months later, we were expecting again. To be sure, I took multiple pregnancy tests. Each result was stronger than the one before. My heart was comforted and hopeful that the miscarriage was a fluke and I would be well on my way to a healthy pregnancy.

I came down with a case of food poisoning a week later. Cramping ensued but I chalked it up to my body's response to the food. It didn't stop. Soon it was accompanied by spotting. My heart wavered. *Surely this can't be happening again.*

The doctor ordered a sonogram and we watched the little life flicker on the screen. The baby's heartbeat was strong but several large clots threatened its viability. Each morning I woke to the question, "Will he or she make it through today?" The bleeding never abated. The following Saturday morning, I hosted a baby shower for my friend at my parents' house. Pink flowers, dresses too tiny to be real, punch-sipping, and baby-gabbing, my thoughts couldn't help but wander to the life struggling inside me. I tried my best to rejoice in my friend's delight but my heart weighed heavy with what seemed inevitable. The cramping and bleeding worsened until I was forced to leave the party early.

I lost the baby. Again.

I named him Elijah even though we never officially knew the sex. I didn't know the meaning of the name until after the fact. The meaning? "My God is Yahweh." My God is I AM WHO I AM. *I AM enough. My grace is sufficient. I AM the LORD of steadfast love. I will never give up on you. I AM for you.*

This time I mourned freely and deeply. I didn't temper it with, "It's okay, we can try again." I let myself feel the loss and find the Lord to be sufficient. It took a bit longer to heal and to ready my heart for trying again. That summer, I lived in the moment and relished our family of four. I learned to say with the psalmist,

Before I was afflicted I went astray,
but now I keep your word.
You are good and do good;
teach me your statutes. (Ps. 119:67–68)

WRESTLING WITH GOD

Before the miscarriages, I presumed upon the Lord's grace in blessing me with children. I reckoned that He would give me what I wanted when I wanted it. I believed that His goodness was dependent upon His dealings with me. If He blessed me, He was good. If He withheld, He was not trustworthy. It was a conditional sort of trust. I didn't have eyes to see His grace and goodness in the good and the bad—in blessing and in suffering. And since I couldn't see His grace as clearly, giving thanks was a stunted practice.

Enter Norah, my third-born. From the day I discovered I was pregnant, fear crouched at every corner. *Would I wake up to bleeding or cramping? Would there be a heartbeat? Will I make it to full term?* I wrestled hard with the Lord. I wrestled with Him like Jacob did.

Jacob was the son of Isaac, the son of Abraham, who cheated his twin brother out of his birthright and blessing. Understandably, his brother, Esau, sought revenge. He threatened to kill Jacob for theft. Jacob sought asylum among his mother's family miles away. Years and wives and children later, he faced an encounter with Esau. He feared for his life. He wasn't sure if time would have healed wounds or caused them to fester gangrenous. The night before he was to meet Esau and confront his past, he found himself alone in the dark:

The same night he arose and took his two wives, his two female servants, and his eleven children, and crossed the ford of the Jabbok. He took them and sent them across the stream, and everything else that he had. And Jacob was left alone. And a man wrestled with him until the breaking of the day. When the man saw that he did not prevail against Jacob, he touched his hip

socket, and Jacob's hip was put out of joint as he wrestled with
him. Then he said, "Let me go, for the day has broken." But Jacob
said, "I will not let you go unless you bless me." And he said to
him, "What is your name?" And he said, "Jacob." Then he said,
"Your name shall no longer be called Jacob, but Israel, for you have
striven with God and with men, and have prevailed." Then Jacob
asked him, "Please tell me your name." But he said, "Why is it
that you ask my name?" And there he blessed him. So Jacob called
the name of the place Peniel, saying, "For I have seen God face to
face, and yet my life has been delivered." The sun rose upon him
as he passed Penuel, limping because of his hip. (Gen. 32:22–31)

Before Jacob's wrestle with God, he presumed upon His grace. The Lord was the God of his father and grandfather. He had yet to become the God of Jacob. Jacob assumed that God's blessing would be on him because it was on the men before him. He was right. God would bless Jacob. And He would make Jacob a blessing to the whole world. The weight of that blessing was yet to be felt by Jacob until he wrestled with the Lord. In His goodness, the Lord left him with a gift—a limp. He afflicted Jacob. He didn't leave him the same. Jacob responded in humility by acknowledging that he shouldn't have even been allowed to live. He saw God face to face and yet was spared. He saw God's grace and responded with gratitude.

The fear of losing another baby positioned me to wrestle with God on my own. This was between the Lord and me. Matt couldn't help. He couldn't wrestle for me. The losses I had already sustained left me with a limp. But that limp reminded me of God's grace. Each morning that I rose to look in the mirror and see my belly growing was a cause to thank God. I knew that I wasn't guaranteed to have the pregnancy turn out like I hoped, but I was grateful the Lord gave me one more day. One more day to dream. One more day to carry this child. One more day to thank Him. I saw His grace, I gave the thanks. Grace. Thanks. Grace. Thanks.

DECIMATION AND RESTORATION

Outside of Matt's cancer, the miscarriages and my pregnancy with Norah were some of the most trying times. Counting God's grace and giving thanks isn't without struggle. But the limp has steadied my heart to know that the Lord is good and does good. It prepared me to face the storm—to trust God with Matt's life and the future of our family. I knew no matter what, God is the God for man—the Lord of steadfast love.

> *He turns rivers into a desert,*
> *springs of water into thirsty ground,*
> *a fruitful land into a salty waste,*
> *because of the evil of its inhabitants.*
> *He turns a desert into pools of water,*
> *a parched land into springs of water.*
> *And there he lets the hungry dwell,*
> *and they establish a city to live in;*
> *they sow fields and plant vineyards*
> *and get a fruitful yield.*
> *By his blessing they multiply greatly,*
> *and he does not let their livestock diminish.* (Ps. 107:33–38)

The end of Psalm 107 can be puzzling and somewhat troubling. Why would God turn rivers to desert, a fruitful land to a salty waste? It seems harsh. We understand and applaud the restoration: His turning the desert into pools of water and letting the hungry dwell in the city. But why the decimation bit? The answer? Both are His grace. Both are evidence of His steadfast love for the children of man. There's a story Jesus tells in Luke 15 of God's grace through decimation and restoration.

A man had two sons. The younger son asked his father for the share of his estate. Normally, his inheritance would not be accessible unless the father died. Being a generous father though, he gave the son what he asked for when he asked for it. He took all that was coming to him and journeyed to a land far away. It didn't take him long to squander his possessions on "reckless living." Verses 14–16 say,

---

And when he had spent everything, a severe famine arose in that country, and he began to be in need. So he went and hired himself out to one of the citizens of that country, who sent him into his fields to feed pigs. And he was longing to be fed with the pods that the pigs ate, and no one gave him anything.

God sent a famine and the son came to his senses. He remembered that even his father's servants fared better. So he arose and headed home, rehearsing his apology all along the way.

The Lord, in His mercy, will dry up our rivers, our wells. He will let us lay our fruitful places to waste so that our "hearts are brought low." He will allow us to suffer the consequences of our folly and struggle through the storm. With our rejoicing and praying spectacles perched on our noses, we can see His grace even there because we know that He is the Lord of steadfast love. We know He is using these circumstances to bring about repentance and reconciliation—for our good and His glory. So we can give Him thanks for the distress—the desert, the chains, folly, and the storm—as much as we thank Him for delivering us from it.

The son's story doesn't end at his journey home. Much to his surprise, his father had been watching the road home anticipating the return of his prodigal son. When the father finally laid eyes on his son, he threw dignity to the wind and raced to meet him. He swallowed him in his arms and kisses. When he could catch his breath, the son said, "Father, I have sinned against heaven and before you. I am no longer worthy to be called your son" (Luke 15:21). His father didn't respond with shame; he didn't dog pile his heartbroken son. Instead, he called the servants to put a robe, a ring, and shoes on his son—to restore him as his child.

God may send a famine; He may dry up our rivers. But He's also the Loving Father who runs toward His sons and daughters even while they are a long way off.

When they are diminished and brought low
through oppression, evil, and sorrow,
he pours contempt on princes
and makes them wander in trackless wastes;
but he raises up the needy out of affliction
and makes their families like flocks.
The upright see it and are glad,
and all wickedness shuts its mouth. (Ps. 107:39–42)

As the father raised up his humiliated son, so God raises His children up out of affliction. The hungry and thirsty, the heavy and broken, the foolish and the storm-soaked find God running toward them, arms wide open, eager to respond with deliverance. After all, He is the God who redeems.

PRAISE

There's one more character in the story of the prodigal son—the older brother. His response to his rebellious sibling is indignant. The father had already given the younger son his inheritance, so what remained was by right the older son's. So the robe, ring, and shoes the father put on the prodigal? Technically, those belonged to the older brother. The food for the feast and wares for the party? The older brother's. The only way the younger brother could be accepted back as a son was at the expense of the older brother.

In the parable of the prodigal son, the older brother acted badly. He resented his father's generosity on his behalf. Rather than joining the celebration for his brother's return, he threw himself a pity party. I probably would have done the same. Praise the Lord, though, we have a better Older Brother.[2]

"For those whom he foreknew he also predestined to be conformed to the image of his Son, in order that he might be the firstborn among many brothers" (Rom. 8:29).

Jesus is the better Older Brother. We are accepted, clothed, and celebrated at His expense. He paid the price for the grace we freely receive. His righteousness covers our unrighteousness. His blood atones for our sin. We walk in the newness of life because we no longer live, but Christ lives in us. And the life we now live in the flesh we live by faith in the Son of God, who loved us and gave himself for us (Gal. 2:20).

His affliction became our admission. All wickedness shuts its mouth because it has no case to bring against us. Christ paid for it.

Such grace? Such thanks in response? It overflows into praise. It's the "let them extol him in the congregation of the people" and the "praise him in the assembly of the elders." The gratitude we feel cannot be contained, it bursts into praise. We acknowledge

God's worth publicly and before those in distinguished positions without fear of what they may think of us. Each of us will have our seasons of the desert, chains, folly, and the storm. None of us are exempt. Whatever station of life, each of us will need deliverance. Each of us will have the chance to see His grace, thank Him for it, and respond in praise.

For those of us who have been in distress and were delivered by the Lord, we have a responsibility to tell it. For the health of our own hearts, the praise must flow forth. As our physical hearts pump oxygenated blood to the rest of the body, so our spiritual hearts pump praise to the Body, the Church—encouraging growth and endurance.

Don't picture "cheerleader" praise, a rah-rah chant and spirit sprinkles. This kind of praise I'm talking about is deep-seated and genuine. It's not for God so that He can "win the game." It's for us and those who hear us. Praise lets us tell on God—to recount all the ways He has been faithful. It's an invitation to join the chorus that has been singing the same song from the beginning:

Whoever is wise, let him attend to these things; let them consider the steadfast love of the Lord.

Conclusion

The journey isn't over. There's still a putting one foot in front of the other. Not all our deserts, prisons, folly, and storms are behind us. They'll come again. But don't let your heart be discouraged. Each season is an opportunity to reveal the anchor of our souls. Are we tethered to that which won't hold? Or, are we chained to the "committed, unchanging, loving determination of the Lord who will never give up on those whom He has chosen for Himself" kind of love?

Maybe you're still in the throes of distress and waiting on His deliverance. Friend, do not give up. He is accomplishing something. He has not turned a deaf ear to you. Some of His deepest and longest-lasting work in me has occurred in the waiting. Rarely was it pretty but I always came out of it more secure in God's steadfast love and with greater affection for and trust in Him. Keep crying out, keep waiting. He will come.

I want to leave you with another psalm (because they're obviously some of my favorite passages in the Bible!). The days leading up to Matt's surgery, a kind man on Twitter pointed me to it. The words wave like a banner in my soul reminding me of the truth that in fearing the Lord, I am blessed and steadied for any season:

Praise the Lord!
Blessed is the man who fears the Lord,
who greatly delights in his commandments!
His offspring will be mighty in the land;
the generation of the upright will be blessed.
Wealth and riches are in his house,
and his righteousness endures forever.
Light dawns in the darkness for the upright;
he is gracious, merciful, and righteous.
It is well with the man who deals generously and lends;
who conducts his affairs with justice.
For the righteous will never be moved;
he will be remembered forever.
He is not afraid of bad news;
his heart is firm, trusting in the Lord.
His heart is steady; he will not be afraid,
until he looks in triumph on his adversaries.
He has distributed freely; he has given to the poor;
his righteousness endures forever;
his horn is exalted in honor.
The wicked man sees it and is angry;
he gnashes his teeth and melts away;
the desire of the wicked will perish!
(Ps. 112, emphasis added)

There's no fear for the one who fears the Lord, for the one whose soul is anchored in His steadfast love. Light dawns in the darkness. The boogeyman beneath the bed is rendered powerless. He is found out to be a pawn in the Lord's hand—a bit player in

God's plan to perfect us as His image bearers, transformed into the likeness of His Son who is "gracious, merciful, and righteous."

Hearing bad news? One's heart may break but it breaks into the hands of the Almighty, All-Sufficient, Loving God—Yahweh, the One who is enough. And even if all does not turn out like we planned, we know this isn't the end. The story is still being written. Christ will return and everything sad will become untrue.[1]

"Behold, the dwelling place of God is with man. He will dwell with them, and they will be his people, and God himself will be with them as their God. He will wipe away every tear from their eyes, and death shall be no more, neither shall there be mourning, nor crying, nor pain anymore, for the former things have passed away." (Rev. 21:3–4)

On this side, we get a glimpse of this. But when the veil is finally lifted? When Jesus comes tearing through the sky? For those who have found the Lord faithful in the desert, prison, folly, and the storm, we will not fear destruction but find awe-filled relief in His return. Come, Lord Jesus, Come!

Epilogue

Closure is something I became acquainted with early in life. One-hundred percent of this is true because of my mother's family's business—Welch Funeral Home. That may sound odd (in more ways than one), but I wouldn't trade my early exposure to death and grief for a more Pollyanna perspective on the "hard" of life.

I remember walking by the state rooms and catching a glimpse of the deceased's profile peeking over the edge of the casket. (Again, I realize this is not typical!) I would ask, "Momma, why do they do that? Why do they put the people in the caskets and then come to look at them?"

She responded, "Closure, baby. They see their loved ones in the casket and know that they're there but not really there. Their bodies are there but what made them *them* isn't. They know their souls have gone on."

For me, her hypothesis has proven true as I've watched grand-parents be put into the ground. Although it was heart-breaking and difficult to see my loved ones in a casket, it brought finality to this life and hope for the life to come for those in Christ.

Closure is good, and my favorite stories come with closure. So now I must apologize because I kept from you an important part of my story that brings a bit of closure. Some of you may have already asked this question. I joyfully supply the answer. But first, the question:

What happened with Matt?

I finished my rough manuscript fully knowing I would have plenty to edit, if not only for the misuse (bordering on abuse) of commas, hyphens, and semicolons, but I hadn't considered that I left you without the current status of my husband. Please accept my deepest apology.

As of today, Matt has been cancer-free for 5 years, 7 months, and 24 days. He receives a scan and sees his neuro-oncologist twice a year to monitor his progress. While we would be delighted to call him "in remission," we were told at his diagnosis that brain tumors are never truly cured. However, we believe in a God who can do the impossible. We ask for and believe that, fully knowing God is able. We put our trust not in Matt's health, but in the Lord of steadfast love.

Notes

Chapter One

1. Will Kynes, "God's Grace in the Old Testament: Considering the Hesed of the Lord," *Knowing & Doing,* C. S. Lewis Institute (Summer 2010). Accessed August 4, 2015.

2. Ibid.

Chapter Two

1. From John Piper, "Job: Reverent in Suffering" sermon, July 7, 1985.

Chapter Three

1. Charles Spurgeon, C. H. *Treasury of David, Psalm 13,* see http://www.spurgeon.org/treasury/ps013.htm. Accessed June 8, 2015.

Chapter Four

1. John Piper, "Can God Spread a Table in the Wilderness?" sermon, November 22, 1981.

2. John Piper, "You Will Never See Death" sermon, May 14, 2011.

3. ESV Study Bible, "Introduction to Hosea."

4. Timothy Keller, "Gospel-Centered Ministry" sermon, May 2007.

Chapter Five

1. C. H. Spurgeon, *The Treasury of David,* see http://www.spurgeon.org/treasury/ps107.htm. Accessed July 8, 2015.
2. C. J. Mahaney, *Humility: True Greatness* (Sisters, OR: Multnomah, 2005), 69.

Chapter Six

1. Gary Thomas, *Sacred Marriage: What If God Designed Marriage to Make Us Holy More Than to Make Us Happy?* (Grand Rapids, MI: Zondervan, 2000).

Chapter Seven

1. In case you aren't hooked on their show on HGTV, Chip and Joanna Gaines host a program called *Fixer Upper* that showcases their renovation talent.

Chapter Eight

1. C. H. Spurgeon, "The Treasury of David," Psalm 107, verse 17.
2. Just so you know, Matt gave me full permission to share this story and what we learned from it. He is a humble and gracious man.

Chapter Nine

1. John Piper, "A Woman Who Fears the Lord Is to Be Praised" sermon, May 10, 1981.
2. ESV Study Bible notes, "Practical Implications of the Incommunicable Attributes of God."
3. The word *pure,* see http://dictionary.reference.com/browse/pure?s=t. Accessed July 7, 2015.

Chapter Ten

1. C. S. Lewis, *The Problem of Pain* (New York, NY: HarperCollins, 2015).

2. J. I. Packer, *Knowing God Through the Year* (Downers Grove, IL: InterVarsity Press, 2004), 81.

3. Beth Moore, *So Long, Insecurity* (Carol Stream, IL: Tyndale House, 2010), 86.

Chapter Eleven

1. Wayne Grudem, *Christian Beliefs: Twenty Basics Every Christian Should Know* (Grand Rapids, MI: Zondervan, 2005), 27.

2. Tim Keller sermon.

Chapter Twelve

1. Karl Barth, *Church Dogmatics*, IV.1.

2. For a wonderfully in-depth perspective on this parable, I whole-heartedly recommend Tim Keller's *Prodigal God* (New York, NY: Penguin Books, 2008).

Conclusion

1. A nod to Sam Gamgee's question to Gandalf in J. R. R. Tolkien's *The Lord of the Rings*.